Finding the God-Dependent Life

Discovery House
P U B L I S H E R S
BOX 3566 · GRAND RAPIDS. MI 49501

*PUBLISHING BOOKS THAT FEED
THE SOUL WITH THE WORD OF GOD.*

Finding the God-Dependent Life:

A Personal Story of a Life Transformed by the Secret of 'God-Dependence' Over Co-dependence

Joanie Yoder

With deepest thanks to Joan—a rare
friend who loves me as Jesus does and
who has prayed this book into existence.

Finding the God-Dependent Life:
A Personal Story of a Life Transformed
by the Secret of God-Dependence Over Co-Dependence

Published first in the United Kingdom by Hodder & Stoughton, Ltd.,
London as *The God-Dependent Life,* copyright © 1991 by Joanie Yoder

This edition copyright © 1992 by Joanie Yoder

Unless indicated otherwise, Scripture quotations are from
the King James Version.

Library of Congress Cataloging-in-Publication-Data

Yoder, Joanie, 1934
Finding the God-dependent life: a story of a life transformed by the
secret of God-dependence over co-dependence / Joanie Yoder
p. cm.

ISBN: 0-929239-62-8

1. Yoder, Joanie, 1934—. 2. Christian biography. I. Title.
BR1725.Y63A3 1992   248.4'092—dc20   92-6246
[B]   CIP

Discovery House Publishers is affiliated with Radio Bible Class,
Grand Rapids, Michigan

Discovery House books are distributed to the trade by
Thomas Nelson Publishers, Nashville, Tennessee 37214

All rights reserved.

Printed in the United States of America

92 93 94 95 / CHG / 10 9 8 7 6 5 4 3 2 1

Contents

Foreword

Joanie Yoder has written about a "long obedience in the same direction." This is not a Cinderella story where problems are solved with wishful thinking and miracle interventions. It is a book ultimately about the faithfulness of God in the midst of real life.

Bill and Joanie have ministered in the midst of troubled youth in situations that most only know about through television documentaries. Their ministry has not been about the easy fix. It is not all pain, but it is not all roses either. This is a book that will speak to today's Christian as Sheldon Van Aukens' *A Severe Mercy* spoke years ago. It is all the more powerful for me because I have been an observer of the whole saga. I watched Bill and Joanie fall in love, I watched their call to missionary service mature, and as a coworker in Youth for Christ I observed and monitored their life of service in Europe.

C. S. Lewis once said, "Not one square inch of the planet is uncontested." This book is about the contest and more particularly Joanie's discovery of the resource of God's presence in the midst of the battle. So many are defeated at this very point as we attempt to serve Christ in a modern world. We are clearly motivated by Christ and the gospel; we understand to some degree the nature and implications of His message; however, we sometimes feel ourselves defeated because we do not fully apprehend the desire of God to be our strength and support.

Joanie Yoder has not spared herself or shielded us from the struggle of Christian service. This is a missionary story both believable and inspiring. For me it also brings closure to some haunting questions about why God's will is sometimes revealed to us in great pain, confusion, and loss. This is a book about incarnation and the desire of God to continue to express Himself through the experience of His people. The places and circumstances are modern; however, their twentieth century context does not make them different or less true than those of the first century. Times, situations, and names have changed, but God remains faithful. This is a modern true-life story, carrying this needed truth right to the center of our hearts. The "shadow of the Almighty" continues to hover over our lives, dreams, and efforts.

Jay Kesler, President
Taylor University

Introduction

This book is the culmination of years—years of hammering out my discovery of the God-dependent life on the anvil of ordinary daily living, years of having it tested and proven in the crucible of struggle, pain, and loss.

It's been said that if we wish to share great lessons of life, it is not enough merely to tell people our conclusions—*we need to share the process that brought us to those conclusions.* That's been my aim in this book. All principles of God-dependence that I have shared in the following chapters have been "fleshed out" with those personal experiences that were used by God to bring me to such an understanding.

Running in and out of these experiences, the not-so-silken thread of my own humanness will be traced by you, the reader. I've no doubt that the inner response of most readers will more than confirm Frederick Buechner's view expressed in his book *The Sacred Journey* "that the story of any one of us is in some measure the story of us all."

Believing this to be so, I dare to hope that my story will be a means of reassurance and hope to all who find themselves in this book. Should this be true for you personally, then my prayer is that the tried-and-tested credibility of each principle shared in these pages will play a dynamic part in restoring God-dependence to your own Christian life and faith, even as it did in mine.

Destination Rock Bottom

1 I felt sickened at what I was about to do. But at least it was the honest thing. As a defeated, down-and-out missionary, honesty seemed the only option left to me now, at least the only option with self-respect. And God knows, I needed all the self-respect I could get.

Gripping a small pair of scissors in my right hand, I opened the cover of my leather Bible with the other. Ah yes, there it was, just as I had remembered—my "life hymn" I had once called it. That was ten years earlier, during my college days, back when it was the fashion to "claim" a favorite Bible verse or hymn and then stake one's entire life and future on it. But it was not so much fashion as a swelling tide of spiritual fervor and heroism inside me that had prompted me to pen this hymn into the front leaf of my Bible. The simple act of recording it seemed to transform it into a document of personal destiny, a destiny as binding, I felt, as the Bible on which it rested. But things had changed since then. For a long time now my so-called life hymn, together with the Bible itself, had lain undisturbed beneath that leather cover like a faded and forgotten photograph.

At the sight of that old, once-cherished hymn, I felt my raw emotions bleed straight down to my fingertips as I stroked them slowly across the page. How meaningfully I had written those lines—and in my very best hand, I noted. How full of faith I remembered feeling at the time, for I had believed with the whole of my young heart that these words, reverenced somehow by all the "Thees" and "Thous", would be the unwavering theme of my entire life and service:

> Let me burn out for Thee, dear Lord,
> Burn and wear out for Thee;
> Don't let me rust or my life be
> A failure, my God, to Thee.
> Use me and all I have, dear Lord,
> And get me so close to Thee,
> That I feel the throb of the great heart of God,
> Until I burn out for Thee.

"Burn and wear out for Thee?" I was feeling worn out all right, and burned out too, all within our first decade of Europe-based ministry, a ministry under Youth for Christ that had taken us first to Frankfurt, Germany, then on to West Berlin, and more recently to Geneva, Switzerland. Following eight grueling years in the divided city of Berlin, Switzerland seemed far more peaceful and picturesque in reality than it was in reputation. Even after two years in Geneva, the contrast between Berlin's political tensions and Switzerland's tranquillity made it hard to believe that this quiet, peace-loving country really was home for our family. Not only that, for the first time in our married life we finally had a standard of living that seemed more in keeping with the culture we were trying to reach. Much to our discomfort, Berliners occasionally had expressed their puzzlement, even embarrassment, over our faded pre-war wallpaper and shabby furnishings. Like most Europeans, they assumed that all Americans were rich.

By the time we got to Geneva, however, our financial support had increased sufficiently so that we had the joy of moving into a modern, nearly-new, fourth-floor apartment. As if that weren't enough, we were blessed with two spacious balconies that overlooked a distant range of mountains, providing a postcard-looking backdrop for watching sleek, silvery aircraft glide in and out of Geneva airport. With an idyllic environment like this, I knew that I should be the happiest American woman and Christian missionary on the face of the earth. But I wasn't. Nowhere near it. "Burned out"—those two words described me to a T. But the question was, what was I burned out *for?* Not for any worthwhile purpose that I could see. Certainly not for *God.*

The scissors were still poised in my hand, rather like a crude surgical instrument waiting to snip away that page of frustrated personal history. Why, then, was I suddenly so reluctant to carry out my decision? After all, I reminded myself, it wasn't as if I were about to cut away a page from the Word of God. And yet my overloaded conscience made me feel as if this were exactly the case.

I heaved a fretful sigh and glanced up from my Bible, perhaps for some emotional relief, perhaps as a bid for time. For a long, drawn out moment I looked through the picture-frame windows of our apartment and out across the valley toward the nearby city of Geneva, out still further to the green foothills of the Swiss mountains, and then across time itself, all the way back to my days at Taylor University, a college situated on the fringe of a quaint, one-horse town known as Upland, Indiana. . . .

Time stood still long enough for me to flick through major scenes of my life, beginning with those life-shaping college days and then being sucked through the downward spiral that had dropped me at this painful present moment. I suppose it was all part of a last-ditch effort to uncover just one good reason for not cutting this hymn out of my Bible, and even more, out of my life.

Standing motionless over my open Bible, my memory telescoped back to those blithe, action-packed college days. But now I was remembering them more for their significance than for their whirlwind of activities, days of callings and leadings, of promises and commitments. My own calling, something I had never doubted for one moment—not even now, oddly enough—was to serve God in some foreign land. Like many with missionary vision in that era, I imagined myself living and working among drum-beating, idol-worshiping tribal people in some remote, far-flung corner of the globe. And so I had dismissed my recurring burden for modern Europe. "Nobody will call *that* a mission field!" was my reasoning, reasoning that was far from groundless. In those days the "in" world view among the most zealous, missionary-minded people was, "No one should hear the gospel twice until everyone has heard it once." In other words, Europe had had its chance. But then, I protested secretly, hadn't America had its chance as well—and was still having it? On the other hand, who was I to question the correctness of those missionary statesmen who had come up with this fair-sounding though hard-to-apply concept?

In the meantime a tall, lanky fellow-student named Bill sauntered into my life and took my heart in one fell swoop. Not that it was love at first sight, far from it, for I had been admiring Bill's many virtues from a slight distance for well over a year. True to his reputation as a disciplined student, majoring in biblical studies and preparing for missionary work, he usually could be seen sitting at the same table in the same corner of the library at about the same time each day. As he sat at that table, single-mindedly studying his notes and a stack of books, little did he realize that a female admirer was sitting nearby, studying him!

True, he had a rather disjointed way of walking (he was fondly known on campus as a person who walked in sections), and he was conspicuously underweight for his height. Yet inside that gangly but handsome form I discerned a man of rare character. Again and again I saw it mirrored attractively in his gentle, brown eyes and even more so in his gentle ways. Without a doubt, here was a man of transparent integrity, a real-life embodiment of that popular song "Just Plain Bill." Before I had spent so much as five minutes in his company, I was conscious of wanting to spend the rest of my life with him.

And then a timely turn of events altered the picture. Out of all the students on campus that might have been selected, Bill and I were thrown together on a committee. In no time at all, he and I formed a secret subcommittee, a "mutual admiration society for two" that progressed quickly from admiration to romance. But ours was not one of those "falling in love with love" sort of romances. Both of us had been through that in earlier relationships, and we knew it wasn't enough. Nor had we merely fallen in love with each other, though we couldn't say that we hadn't. It's just that it went further than that, almost as if our love had come to us first of all as a gift from above to be received and unwrapped, perhaps one of those marriages said to be made in heaven. All we knew was that God was at the heart of our relationship, and that fact seemed to take us beyond simply falling in love, or for that matter, ever falling out of it. Ours was a realistic love, I remembered thinking, a love that reckoned on our fair share of frightening unknowns to be faced in the future, yet secure enough in its source to cast out the fear.

This love for each other, plus Bill's clear call to serve the Lord after graduation among Germany's post-war youth, together with his whispered, "Joanie, will you marry me?" all added up to more than enough guidance to confirm my burden for Europe. My response to Bill's proposal came from a heart with all the stops pulled out, but with a voice so choked up with ecstasy that it could hardly find utterance. "You *know* that I will!" I squeaked unromantically. "What did you say?" Bill asked equally unromantically, with a stunned expression on his face. He had heard only the word "know" and thought I had said "no." And so once more, this time with a voice loosened up with a burst of laughter, I repeated the words he was longing to hear: "Bill, honey, you know that I will!"

Still letting my mind move across the months and years, the changing scenes of time drew me from that unforgettable evening of proposal to its natural outcome— our candle-lit wedding the following March in 1956. For a moment I recaptured the tenderness of that ceremony, remembering the total devotion reflected in our eyes as we spoke our vows to each other: "For better, for worse . . . for richer, for poorer . . . in sickness and in health . . . till death us do part." Because we wanted our marriage altar also to be an altar of dedication to serve the Lord with our entire lives, we had adapted our ceremony thoughtfully around this dual commitment. At the end of our vows, with snow and wind swirling outside the church and the warm glow of candlelight creating a stillness within, Bill and I sealed our consecration in the presence of our misty-eyed witnesses by singing a prayer to the One who had brought us together. Losing the sense of all else but ourselves and God and that altar, we sang our humble duet for His ears alone: "Have Thine own way, Lord, have Thine own way, Thou art the Potter, we are the clay."

Our scenic wedding trip through the Blue Ridge Mountains came and went, and then melted into miles and miles of deputation meetings in a variety of churches and states. At last our support needs were met, just in time for us to board a grand-looking passenger vessel in Quebec, Canada, heading for Europe. It was early June when we stood on deck, throwing our last kisses and waving both arms in farewell to a huddle of beloved family members waving back to us from a receding pier. As we launched farther and farther out to the open seas, I knew beyond a shadow of doubt that the assignment of this ship was not merely to carry us off to Germany; it was carrying us straight into the lofty, heroic purposes of our future lives. Bill was twenty-two when we arrived in Germany; I was twenty-one and two months into pregnancy. The sum total of our possessions consisted of several donated antique chests jammed full of wedding presents—crisp floral sheets, some to be hung as our first curtains, big fluffy "his" and "her" towels, an assortment of valuable knick-knacks, plus a few old treasures tucked in with our favorite, dog-eared books. Most basic of all was our dinky washing machine with a hand wringer, a weird and wonderful contraption that could wash only one sheet at a time! All these were the means of civilizing our first home, a primitive rented room in a partially bombed-out building in the least desirable part of Frankfurt.

Bill spoke beginner's German, and I spoke none, but we would learn—Bill through sermon preparation and study, and I, for a start, through venturing into local shops with well-practiced shopping lists, the one thing I learned to do well. We were happy, that's all—young, happy, and visionary. Part of my personal happiness was the prospect of the two of us turning that corner of the world upside-down for God. Naturally it would take time, I had reminded myself, consciously trying to temper my idealism with a fair amount of realism. But together we would do it. After all, not only did we serve a great God, but at my side was big, strong, adequate Bill.

Not until years later, given the chance to look back through the refocused lens of hindsight, would I recognize that this was exactly where it all began to slip and slide. Didn't I notice, for instance, that I was beginning to depend less and less on God and more and more on big, strong, adequate Bill? Didn't I see the connection between my transferred dependence on Bill and my waning appetite for Bible reading, meditation, and prayer, an uncomfortable dryness of spirit that disturbed me deeply? No, indeed I did not! All I knew was that the demands of married life and missionary life were bringing me face to face with my inadequacies for the first time ever. Deep down I always knew they were there, but my protected background and streamlined college life had enabled me to live as if they weren't. Now "real life" in all its seriousness had begun for me, and nothing I had experienced so far had prepared me for it. No longer could I squeeze through on the strength of a bubbly personality and the ability to "act as if." I simply couldn't dodge my inadequacies any longer. But neither could I bear to admit them to anyone else, not even to myself. That's when I began to discover, to my great relief, just how invincible my six-foot-three husband could be, invincible enough for both of us, it seemed to me. And my gut-level lack of confidence only served to encourage this lopsided arrangement. Again, not until much later would I recognize that what started out as proper interdependence within marriage gradually had turned into an improper dependence on my part: *husband*-dependence instead of *God*-dependence.

By and by my husband-dependence became such a pattern that I found myself evading anything and everything untried or new to my experience and simply letting Bill handle things. "Still, that's probably why I've been given Bill," I rationalized each time I gave in to my lack of confidence, avoiding some reasonable challenge or a chance to stretch my abilities and grow—such as figuring out the bus and subway system, or better yet, learning to drive so that I could assist Bill or get out there and do a few things for myself. Of course, the fact that Bill appeared to do it all so easily only reinforced my sense of inadequacy, giving me the impression that *he* had something going for him that I simply didn't have.

To my further relief, my tendency to let Bill cover for me obviously suited him as much as it did me. Apart from Bill's preference to do most things himself anyway, especially if it saved the bother of explaining how someone else might do them, I noticed that he almost *needed* to cover for me in this way as a regular, reassuring proof of his manliness and sense of responsibility. For better or for worse (and initially it probably was a bit of each), it was clearly the assumption of us both that this is what good, strong Christian husbands were ordained to do for the "weaker sex."

But time and life marched relentlessly on in my reflections, bringing still another scene of the past in front of me. In 1958, a year and a half after our arrival in Germany, we moved from Frankfurt to West Berlin, that famous sector known back then as an "island of freedom," proudly holding its own 110 miles behind the iron curtain. This divided city with its teeming population of searching youth would be our absorbing mission field for the next few years; and our enormous, uncarpeted apartment would become known for its volume of "wall-to-wall young people," as we fondly called them.

This move was a family move, for now we were three. Christina, named after my Swedish grandmother, was like a petite little Goldilocks straight out of my childhood storybooks. I was already pregnant again, quite a bit sooner than hoped, but happily nonetheless. Then shortly before Christmas, as temperatures fell and dropped a blanket of snow on Berlin, I began to hemorrhage severely. Within minutes I was rushed to a hospital where English was spoken. For several days I lay in a hospital bed and continued to bleed, hoping with everyone else that it would stop and the pregnancy would be saved. But on and on I bled until finally, in favor of saving at the very least my own life, an emergency operation was carried out. While I slept the sleep of injections and ether, that second little soul within me —Tiny Tim we later called him—had the shock of seeing the light of day two months too soon, weighing only two and a half pounds.

As I lay on the operating table, emerging from the anesthetic and waking up to the pain, my eyes watched doctors and nurses busying themselves with everything and everyone else but me. I waited and waited, patiently at first, for someone to acknowledge my presence and to show me our son. Soon I began to feel less and less like a mother and more like a malfunctioned baby machine, shoved to one side to be dealt with when convenient.

From somewhere underneath my newly sewn incision a muzzled, silent scream wanted to cry out, "How can you be so unfeeling, so inhuman?" Not once was our newborn son brought near, not once was I permitted to feel his velvety skin against mine, not once was I given the chance to cradle him in my arms.

At long last I was permitted one fleeting glimpse of his tiny face peering over a bundle of blankets, but only from a painful distance. He was being held (and clearly *withheld)* in the arms of a stern-looking nurse who had planted herself resolutely in the opposite corner of the operating room. Reaching out my aching arms toward her, I pleaded in halting German, "Bitte . . . bitte." (Please . . . please.) But all she said in return was a flat "Nein . . . Nein." (No . . . no.) Then she turned and whisked him away, away in a taxi I was informed as I demanded to know where she was taking him, bound for a distant children's hospital that seemed as far away from me as the far side of the moon. Why hadn't they warned us that this hospital wasn't equipped with incubators, I demanded to know further in utter disbelief. But to this question I received no answer at all.

Miles away from us, in a hospital on the other side of West Berlin, Tiny Tim's perfect little form fought all alone for his life. Thirty hours later he finally weakened and died, not of premature birth we were told, but sadder still, of pneumonia —quite understandable considering his unprotected winter journey the day before. Our last chance of ever holding our baby, dead or alive, was given away for good as Bill and I made the split-second decision to sign over his body to be used in medical research.

During the next few days, days that stretched over

Christmas, Bill and I comforted each other at my hospital bed by sharing wordless grief together, for it was more than a "premie" we had lost; we had lost a son that had been born, had lived and had died, all within an eternity of thirty hours. Christmas that year was hardly a season for being jolly, though in a way it was our first *real* Christmas. Certainly it was our first glimpse of God's original Christmas when He too suffered empty arms because of a far-away Son born to die. My young motherheart throbbed as only a mother's heart can beneath my rising unsuckled milk. My very womb, recovering from the Caesarean section ached with the loss, an ache that stood little chance of subsiding as miscarriage was to follow miscarriage in our attempts to enlarge our family circle.

I remembered thinking one day, *My womb is beginning to feel like a graveyard.* It wasn't that I was embittered over my multiple losses, nor was I angry with anyone, least of all with God, though there were those who thought I ought to have been. No, on that day when I was brought the news that our Tiny Tim had died (until that moment it hadn't crossed my mind that he might not live), I found myself giving the same response that Job did when he learned of the loss of his children: "The LORD gave, and the LORD hath taken away; blessed be the name of the LORD" (Job 1:21). Saying those words with all of my heart had been an act of relinquishment, a response that enabled me to experience the depths of grief without bitterness.

But instead of bitterness, I became aware of something else just as destructive hammering away at my emotions. Miscarriage after miscarriage, a growing sense of physical failure began to build up inside me, and with it an accumulation of guilt toward all those little ones whom I had conceived, carried, and loved, but had failed to bring to birth. In short, buried inside me was an acute sense of *shame.*

But my inner shame was soon to be overshadowed by

Berlin's infamous "Wall of Shame," erected overnight by East German Communists in 1961 while the city slept. How outraged we felt, waking up to the news that East and West had been alienated still further, with the crude materials of cement and barbed wire being used to separate family and friends, among them dear friends of ours. Some time later, Bill had stood among the masses that crammed into the city square to see and hear John F. Kennedy as he recharged the flagging spirits of the entire Berlin population with his electrifying words: "Ich bin ein Berliner!" ("I am a Berliner!")

In the meantime I had been nursing yet another pregnancy that hung in the balance week after discouraging week. Finally I dared move from my bed, then from room to room in slow motion, and gradually out into a cautious but hopeful build-up to a normal full-term birth at last in 1963. As Bill and I cradled our beautiful, brown-eyed daughter in our arms, overcome by the sheer disbelief that comes with a miracle, another little storybook maiden came to mind. As a child I had read and re-read the well-loved Heidi of the Alps books and had always dreamed of having a Heidi of my own. Without much ado, that became the chosen name for this precious gift, sent to us six years after Christina's birth.

With the addition of Heidi, we were now an ideal four. At last life would begin to normalize. Or would it? I was beginning to find out what it was like to be one of those who "labour and are heavy laden," our Lord's own description of people like me in Matthew 11:28. My big, strong, adequate Bill, perhaps no longer soaring on wings like an eagle, was running nonetheless like a trained athlete and *not* growing weary, or at least not admitting to it. Just occasionally I had tried to slow the runner down by luring him to the sidelines for a few minutes of after dinner hand-holding and whispered "sweet nothings" on the sofa. But Bill found it hard to relax, day or night, until the work was done. And naturally the work was never done. So a quick hug and a single-minded, "Gotta keep moving!" was always his reply, a reply that eventually became a humorous by-word in our household, mischievously used by all of us, even by Bill himself!

In the light of Bill's tireless, marathon spirit, my best option was to try to keep up with him. If I couldn't be close to Bill apart from work, then I would seek to be close to him within it. And this I sought to do until we were operating like a pair of Siamese twins. Bill would bring home crowds of young people, and I would cook for them; Bill would preach in our meetings, and I would accompany hymn-singing on the piano; I would sing solos, and Bill would accompany me on the piano; I would design and draw artwork for advertising, and Bill would print it on our own offset printing machine. Side by side we would go on working until late each evening without rest or relief, except for falling into bed and "dying" for a few hours at night. For years our sole leisure activity was an occasional late-night stroll to the nearby mail box where we would post a stack of letters that had taken all evening to write. And for me, all this came in addition to looking after home and family.

On the surface of things, I appeared to be keeping in stride with Bill and his roadrunner lifestyle. But on the inside, I was feeling on the verge of collapse, feeling guilty that I found it so hard to keep up, and feeling strangely alone, even as a Siamese twin. All the blood, sweat, and tears of only a few years were taking their toll on my delicate frame, and I was weary to the core—pregnancy-weary, ministry-weary, and just plain life-weary.

It's not that things were so much harder than anticipated when we first started out. After all, weren't these tough experiences our "fair share of frightening unknowns" that I had anticipated even before our marriage? Yes, they were. And yes, I really had counted on hardships; I really had dedicated myself to enduring them with Bill and to winning over them through faith. The one frightening unknown I hadn't counted on facing, however, was *the exhausting hardship of my own human inadequacy,* plus the additional hardship of maintaining all the necessary pretense and instinctive escape mechanisms I had acquired in order to give a reasonable guise of coping. These I had grown to hate even more than my inadequacies. I simply was not the conquering Joan of Arc I had hoped to be, nor would Bill forever be invincible enough for both of us.

I must no longer expect Bill to cover for me, I inwardly decided one day. *I must become stronger . . . I must try harder . . . I must do better . . . I must trust the Lord more—* all said with teeth-clenching emphasis on the letter I. But instead of putting my trust in the Lord, I was putting it elsewhere—less in Bill, to be sure, but now much more in myself. Oddly enough, I remained totally oblivious to this fact, blatant though it was. My "try harder" brand of Christianity not only encouraged self-trust under the guise of self-sacrifice, it also blinded me to its part in my emotional distress, which by now was becoming so great that I sometimes felt I was losing my mind. Though all human strength, physical and mental, was ebbing away, I managed to resuscitate it for the umpteenth time by reviving my resolve to carry on more admirably. But for how long? And what then? This was my latest ever-present anxiety.

"Bill . . ." I asked him one day, trying to broach the subject with calm concern in spite of overwhelming feelings to the contrary, ". . . do you ever wonder if I'm on the verge of a nervous breakdown?" Several times I had come to him with this question, and each time, hardly glancing up from his work, Bill would reply without a hint of worry (or hadn't he let on?) "Naahh, of course not, honey! Don't you worry, you're going to be okay!" Reassuring words, but they were getting harder every day to believe.

What a shame to my calling that it hadn't occurred to

me that I might have gone to *God* and asked *Him* if I were about to have a nervous breakdown. But I hadn't learned to come to Him with personal failure, not yet at least, for I hadn't counted on such glaring failure, certainly not as a Christian worker and not as Bill's wife. What I *had* learned, even if I hadn't meant to, was the self-sufficient trait of going to God more and more as a last resort and, therefore, only in critical moments, particularly when feeling near to my breaking point. Using prayer as a sort of panic button, I would physically stop in my tracks, as if momentarily jumping off the treadmill of life itself, and lift my eyes heavenward. Scouring around inside myself for a mustard seed of faith, I would freeze where I was and in a desperate whisper would claim the gift of peace promised by Jesus in John's gospel: "Peace I leave with you; my peace I give you. I do not give to you as the world gives. Do not let your hearts be troubled and do not be afraid" (John 14:27 NIV). Then I would unfreeze, and "stepping out in faith," I would go my way a little less troubled and less afraid.

Time and again, like a walking, talking doll whose batteries had run down, I would recharge myself in this way to tide me over. Day after agonizing day I somehow managed to keep plodding on and keep giving people that rejoicing-in-the-Lord sort of look as part of being "a good testimony" to others. All the while I kept myself attractively dressed up on the outside but felt myself getting more and more messed up on the inside. A few small tokens of peace, quickly spent, simply were not enough. I was in need of total renovation, for I was beginning to feel old before I had hit thirty. Or did I only wish I were old?

Finally there was one last scene coming into view, a scene from the more recent past: our move to Switzerland in 1964. It all began with Bill's return from our organization's staff conference and his news that he had been appointed as its new European director. For some time I had sensed change in the air, a merciful insight sent from the Lord, I believed, to prepare me for this news and for our move to Geneva, the home of our European headquarters. Leaving Berlin would be a wrench, almost like desertion, we felt. For we would be leaving behind so many friends on both sides of that ugly wall, which, in keeping with political agreement, at least had remained open to those of us with American passports. Nonetheless, the prospect of living in beautiful Switzerland, the land of Bill's own family roots, was a refreshing one. It had made us both feel younger again!

It was a long haul before our move from Berlin to Geneva was complete, but as we finally began to settle into our lovely fourth-floor apartment, I couldn't help thinking that this move, even with all its radical adjustments (such as having to learn French), was possibly the answer to the problem of *me. Now,* since we no longer had a local ministry, I would have time to read my Bible and pray by the hour if I so desired. *Now,* with more rest and less work, I would start feeling better. *Now,* with a smaller, more modern apartment to look after, keeping on top of my responsibilities would be an easy matter. Of course I would miss Bill since he now would need to make extended trips to various European countries, bringing oversight and counsel to the Youth for Christ ministry in each place. But in his absence, the girls and I would be looking forward to Bill's homecomings and our times of togetherness. Instead of pining, we would keep ourselves occupied devising ways to put quality into our treasured times together by a variety of long-planned surprises. At last I was on my way to becoming the happiest American woman on the face of the earth.

Flitting from room to room like a mother bird, I had arranged and rearranged furniture with the renewed energies of plain and simple encouragement. All the while I was thinking of our years in Berlin and doing a bit of self-analysis: perhaps it was only that I'd been depressed by the grayness of the inner-city environment and by those suffocating East German boundaries that encircled the entire western sector. At every border crossing, we stood the chance of being detained and interrogated at length, something we had gone through a number of times; and whenever we needed to travel to West Germany by road, we had to obtain permission from the East German government, buying from them a special visa and often having to justify being civilian residents in Berlin. Hanging over this beautiful, bustling city, and hanging over us, had been a heavy cloud, a stifling atmosphere of confinement, making the phrase "island of freedom" a sheer mockery.

But in direct contrast, that expansive view from our Geneva apartment was like a visual aid, an eloquent reminder of how free we now were—free as the very hills, valleys, and mountains that beckoned us to explore them, free as the wide open skies above and the birds that soared in them. Peace at last, I had thought.

Peace, my foot! I don't know whether I actually said it or whether I only felt like saying it, but that blunt bit of commentary spilled out of my mind and rolled over me like a wave, sweeping me back to the present moment, back to my open Bible and the words, "Let me burn out for Thee." Hot tears started pouring down my cheeks and dangled on my chin. I wiped them away awkwardly with a shoulder, my one hand still gripping the scissors, the other one gripping my open Bible. Everything was blurred except for one clear fact: all my high hopes had collapsed one by one. Two years after our move to Geneva, with all the time in the world, I still wasn't reading my Bible or praying, except for the addition of "prayer cycles" that were one grade up from my usual "panic prayers." After two entire years of more rest and less work, I was feeling worse instead of better. The excitement of Bill's times at home had degenerated into disappointment as I watched him live out of his suitcase and fill daytimes and evenings with preparations for the next trip. Afraid of displeasing Bill as much as displeasing the Lord, I never once voiced my feelings. Instead, trip after trip, I internalized them, burying a growing resentment, not because Bill had been away for five or six weeks, but because he still wasn't with us, not *really* with us, during his five or six days at home.

I was tired of giving and giving and ever more giving with so little in return. And furthermore, I no longer wanted to burn and wear out, not even for the Lord—not yet at least, not until I learned something about real living. Bearing the strain of having an absentee husband and doubling as mother *and* father eight months of the year, I felt ill-prepared to be the sole manager of our home and family life and even less prepared to be satisfied with leftovers. *I wanted something for myself after all!* At last I was admitting something real, even if it didn't sound very noble.

I had searched my memory to find one good reason for not cutting this hymn out of my Bible, but apparently there was none. I couldn't stand my stinking hypocrisy any longer. As I lowered the tip of my scissors and guided the page between the blades, ready to begin cutting, the Lord suddenly intervened sharply, breaking into the situation like a streak of lightning. With swift precision, a split second swifter than the scissors in my hand, He spoke urgently within my barren heart. *"Leave it alone,"* He called out to me. *"Let me change you instead!"* It was the Lord Himself, I knew it, for the words bore His authority. Oddly enough, I answered Him nothing, absolutely nothing. As if in silent agreement, I simply closed my Bible and put the scissors away.

Following the scissors incident, nothing changed for the better that I could see. In fact, matters grew considerably worse. I was on a trip nobody wants to take—the trip downward—and I couldn't shift into reverse for the life of me. But God had begun to deal with that nameless bit of myself that was damaging me, first by His proposal to change me, and then by letting things simply take their course. His love took the risk of seeming not to care or even to be listening as He consented to my downward spiral. I was heading for a breakdown of a certain sort: the breakdown of my pitiful self-sufficiency. I was getting blessedly near to hitting rock bottom and finding out that the rock is *Christ*!

Refashioned Clay

2 By this time I was living with an embarrassing secret, one which only Bill and I knew about. As a result of being rushed to the local doctor one frightening afternoon in the throes of severe heart palpitations, I had been prescribed a short course of tranquilizers and was now swallowing three hefty ones a day. It grieved me deeply that I had come to this; I felt guilty and ashamed before God, a complete write-off in His eyes.

A Christian shouldn't have to resort to tablets for the nerves, I reproached myself harshly, *especially a Christian worker.* But when the pills ran out, I found myself going back for more. "Mother's little helpers" was the cynical way the Rolling Stones would describe such pill taking in one of their rock-and-roll hits a few years later. And I had to admit it, the tranquilizers *did* help. They did bring me a measure of relief, but only at the high price of making me feel afraid to be without them—an early sign of dependence.

Lord, I earnestly prayed one day as I was about to gulp down another one, *I know these pills are not the answer. They deal only with my symptoms, but not the cause of my symptoms. Please deal with the cause so I'll be well and no longer need these wretched things!* As I washed the pill down I had a fleeting but noticeable impression that I had been heard. Or was it only a bit of wishful thinking playing tricks on my emotions, I wondered in typical self-doubt. Then the scissors incident, nearly forgotten, flashed back into my mind and I remembered the ray of hope I had been given that day. Now, perhaps, I was being given an added confirmation of the Lord's clear intention to change me. Nonetheless, my fretting continued to be greater than my faith. How long would it be, I wondered, until I was given more than just the Lord's promise? When and how was He going to change me? What was He waiting for? What was happening to me? Was this a breakdown? Or was it only a "near" breakdown? Would I get better? Would I get worse? What was to become of me?

These questions tussled with each other endlessly in my troubled mind, usually immobilizing me from prayer altogether, but sometimes causing me to devise elaborate prayer schemes that went something like this: first, to ensure that there would be no obstacles to answered prayer, I would confess all my known sins to God; then I would make appropriate promises to Him about living a better Christian life, including renewing the disciplines of prayer and Bible reading; this was followed by boldly claiming scriptural promises concerning God hearing and answering prayer. Finally I would make my usual heartfelt petition, *And now, Lord, please heal me!* At this point I would take on an attitude of expectancy. I honestly wouldn't have been surprised if I had been healed instantly at the sound of my "Amen." But I also was prepared to give it some time. One day and one night would pass, and then another and another. Soon I knew that I wasn't being healed and wouldn't be healed, at least not at the present time. And so I would brace myself and carry on a bit longer— until my next prayer effort, prompted by another point of desperation.

Unsuccessful prayer cycles came and went, and then I came up with the idea of making it more definite by writing it all down thoughtfully on a piece of paper. Line by line I recorded my full confession, listing my own renewed promises alongside scriptural promises, and then in bold letters I stated my petition. Adding the date to it, I held it up before the Lord in prayer, rather like Hezekiah in the Old Testament had done with a letter he had received. For many days after my pact with God, I would refer to my written record again and again as a persistent reminder to Him and a way of reinforcing my faith. But in the end I discarded my paper in a drawer, for I still remained unhealed.

One night I came to a scary end of my own resources and felt myself spiral down to a point I had hoped I never would reach—rock bottom. There was no particular crisis that had triggered it, except that Bill had just left on a nine-week trip to Norway after only a brief stay at home between trips. By then I was living in a constant state of anxiety, and the thought of being alone for such a long stretch was quite daunting.

Fortunately, the girls were tucked in bed sound asleep, as was most of Geneva. I also was in bed but was painfully awake, shaking and shuddering from head to foot with a fit of nerves and clutching my sanity for all it was worth. It was something I had suffered countless times before, but this time it seemed too much to bear. I hadn't the heart nor the will to retrieve my piece of paper and hold it up before the Lord, let alone engage myself in a full-blown prayer cycle. With the mattress itself shuddering beneath me, I informed God in no uncertain terms, *I'd rather have cancer than this!* And I meant every word of it. Then while I felt I had His attention, I began to question God in Job-like fashion, something I had never dared before: *Lord, why haven't you answered my prayer for healing? Just tell me the reason. It's not as if I've asked you to heal a broken leg; I've been asking you to heal my broken personality. Surely that's not hard for you, surely it's your will. To my dying day, Lord, I shall believe that you are the prayer-hearing and prayer-answering God you say you are. So then —just tell me—why don't you answer my prayer? It's not a bitter question; I only want to know the reason.*

In that very instant a thought came to me. Yes, it literally came to me. Although it was my own mind doing the thinking, I was clearly being prompted from beyond myself. The silent influence of the Holy Spirit had passed gently into my distraught mind, turning my attention outward and projecting it across the world, causing me to think aloud to myself: "There must be hundreds . . . no, thousands . . . no, millions of people out there just like me, suffering right this minute just as I am!" For the very first time in my long, dark tunnel of inner suffering, I felt a true burden for others that was greater than my burden for myself. Out of that burden came a spontaneous prayer from my lips, one that was similar yet different from my previous prayers: "Lord, please heal me in such a way that I can bring that same healing to some of those hurting people!"

The choice of words, "heal me in such a way," had been intentional. In that brief moment of time between receiving my new burden and voicing my new prayer, I had reasoned like this: even if God were to heal me instantly as I had first hoped—and I still believed He had the *power* to do so—on what basis could I promise other sufferers the same split-second experience? What if God, who understands us better than we understand ourselves, wished to choose a less dramatic way to bring us even more profound healing? No, the healing I now was seeking would be just as supernatural at its source as the once-for-all instantaneous sort; it still would be God at work and therefore no less effective. But it could be appropriated "in such a way" (and I was still to find out what that way was) that it would be available to every such sufferer as I.

No sooner had I prayed that greater prayer than something passed over me, soft as a summer breeze. It was warm and gentle, like a breath of God assuring me that *this* prayer was the one He intended to answer. There at rock bottom I found out that Christ indeed was the rock on which I had been thrown. I found out that He is not only a prayer-hearer and a prayer-answerer; He is also a *prayer-giver.* The essence of my self-inspired prayer had been, "Lord, heal me"—period. The essence of this Spirit-inspired prayer was, "Lord, heal me *so that . . .*" Although my previous prayer was not wrong, its answer would have affected mainly me, which was as far as my intentions had gone originally. My new prayer, on the other hand, was infinitely greater, for its answer would not only affect me, it would equip me to affect others.

The next morning I felt no better than I had the night before. But for once I wasn't particularly surprised or disappointed. What I felt like at the present moment was no longer so important, for it was only a matter of time until improvement would come, even if I didn't know how. One thing was clear: somewhere up the road ahead of me there would be people waiting for what the Lord had equipped me to offer them, and I had to be ready.

And yet how unlikely that readiness appeared to be as time went on, for I still saw no signs of getting better. I tried to be patient as I waited for this different sort of healing, the sort with which I could cooperate. In my fragile faith I sometimes wondered if my newfound hope had come too late, for my inner tension was already bringing on more disturbing symptoms of distress. At mealtimes every mouthful of food seemed to stick in my throat, causing me to eat less and gradually weigh less. For some time I had felt uneasy, even panicky, about going out and doing ordinary things, particularly my grocery shopping. (I was quite naive, for I had never heard of agoraphobia, the dread of open spaces, which often includes any place outside the walls of one's own home. It hadn't occurred to me that I was experiencing something with a name attached to it.) I was now so daunted by the least responsibility that even a small pile of dishes in the kitchen sink seemed a more mountainous task than climbing the nearby Alps.

The real shame of it all was not that I had all these symptoms, but that no one else knew about them except me. The age of "letting it all hang out" hadn't been heard of yet. One could admit to cancer, heart ailments, a fall down the stairs, or a slipped disc, but not to being a bag of nerves, especially as a Christian and a Christian worker. Oh, how monotonous, even maddening, that line of reasoning had become. What an unnecessary stranglehold those two facts of life had placed on me. Christian and Christian worker! These two life-features should have been my obvious advantages leading me out into spiritual liberation. Instead they had held me captive like two merciless prison guards, making sure I stayed locked up inside myself.

My firm resolve to keep Bill from knowing the full extent of my mounting distresses wasn't difficult to manage in view of his traveling life. That was the only side of our painful separation that suited me, for in spite of God's promise to change me and to heal me, I still couldn't seem to kick one particular fear—the overriding fear that Bill might sense my life grinding to a practical halt and feel forced out of the ministry because of me, or that God Himself might decide to put my disappointing life on a shelf and find someone else to fulfill the things He had wanted me to do, the ultimate failure. I was still in need of further assurance, it seemed.

In an effort to make some sort of sense out of this battle between fear and faith, I began to consider the link between my present nagging fear and one of my childhood fears, happily a much healthier one. When I was still quite young, I possessed a fairly heightened sense of God-awareness, considering my age and my minimal religious knowledge. In my cozy attic bedroom, usually in my bed at night, I often fought sleep off, as children will, by doing a few mental gymnastics about eternity and other deep subjects. The darkness surrounding my bed never seemed frightening or empty. For me, that darkness had become like a friendly, familiar corner of the universe, and in this secret corner I had come to a certain sort of knowing. With all my being, I simply knew there was *God*—not merely *a* God I had decided, but *the one true* God, who had created everything that exists, including me. I knew equally well that this almighty God must have created all things for a purpose, and again that included me. My philosophizing always led me to the same conclusion: since God had created everything and everybody with a purpose, then the worst thing that could happen to any life—to my life—would be to grow up, grow old, and die without ever finding that purpose. It was this thought that would cause a searching sort of fear to envelop me and pull me to my knees. There at my bedside, bowed down with life-and-death matters at such a tender age, I would plead tearfully with that God out there: "Please, please don't let me die without finding your purpose for creating me!" Only then would peace return, allowing me to crawl back into bed and drift off to sleep like any other child.

    Those nights turned into days, the days into weeks and months, and then on into teenage years. By the time I was seventeen, God began to move in closer, using the Christian witness of other teenagers in my high school to get through to me. Being the deeply religious person that I was, and now thoroughly caught up in the activities of the church, I hadn't doubted for one moment that I was already a Christian—not until I began rubbing shoulders with these Christian teens who possessed an "elusive something" I simply didn't have. The more I listened to them speak about the Lord in personal terms (they spoke of having "received the Lord," something I had never heard of) and the more I attended their Youth for Christ rallies, the more I experienced doubt concerning my own Christian understanding. In spite of my deep religious feelings and my sincere attempt to live by them, my Christianity amounted to little more than making sure my good deeds outweighed my bad, and I began to doubt that I was a real Christian at all. These doubts were necessary, of course, for they were helping me to get *un*converted from my superficial Christianity so that I might be converted at last to Christ Himself and to that longed-for purpose in my life.

Finally my moment of truth came. But it wasn't during one of those Saturday-night youth rallies that I always found so stirring. No, God's truth began to dawn in my heart one quiet evening spent at home alone. Feeling rather bored and with nothing better to do, I sat down at the piano and began playing one hymn after another. Prior to that evening I had reached a spiritual impasse because of two unresolved problems in my thinking. The first problem came to my attention every time I heard someone say that Jesus *had* to die on the cross. Inwardly I would think, *Well, He needn't have died, as far as I was concerned. I didn't ask Him to die. I would have believed on Him simply because of His great love and power. He needn't have gone to the extent of* death *to get me to believe in Him.*

The other problem had to do with *repentance*, another word I was hearing rather a lot of. My problem was this: I simply didn't feel any need to repent, though I honestly wished that I could. The fact that I tended to compare myself with those I considered real sinners—thieves, murderers, drunkards, and the like—didn't help, for I always came out looking pretty good and feeling more grateful than repentant.

As I played one of my favorite old gospel hymns, I began reading the words: "Softly and tenderly Jesus is calling, calling for you and for me. . . . Though we have sinned He has mercy and pardon, pardon for you and for me." I stopped playing. "Pardon for you and for *me.*" There it was again—implied repentance. Suddenly, for the first time in my life, instead of comparing myself with others I was being led to compare myself with God Himself. What a revelation that was! Next to God and His unapproachable holiness, I didn't come out so well. I saw myself as unclean and totally unacceptable. There was only one thing to do, and I *wanted* to do it. Repent!

As I rushed up the stairs to my little attic room, I suddenly understood why Jesus *had* to die. He hadn't died merely to impress the likes of me with His love. When Jesus died—it hit me halfway up the stairs—He was accepting on our behalf the punishment for all sin, for *my* sin, the sin which was bringing me to sincere repentance at last.

The moment I reached my room I knelt at my bedside as I had done many times before. But this time it was different. This time I thanked God with a believing heart that Jesus had died for me. For the first time ever I asked Him to forgive me and cleanse me. And then, in all simplicity, I too "received the Lord" by inviting Him to enter my life and to dwell within me forever. That evening that marked my conversion to Christ also marked the moment I ceased striving over the purpose for which I had been created. As I rose from my knees, I remembered thinking, *I still haven't a clue what the purpose is, but that doesn't matter anymore because now I've got the key to that purpose: I've got Christ!* At the same time I was conscious of a blessed bonus —I had come to Christ early in my life, rather than at its end.

This bonus of finding Christ at a young age was illustrated to me one day soon after my conversion as I walked home from school. An avid nature lover, I stopped to finger the supple stems of a young sapling that had been planted near the edge of the road. Lightly touching it, I noticed how agreeably it turned and bent under the slightest pressure of my hand. In my imagination I looked far into the future life of this sapling and I saw a tree—matured, trained, and fixed in some comely form, exactly as desired by the one tending it. I was inspired by this visual aid. Then and there, with nature as my witness, I made a vow to God: I would make sure that I yielded myself under His purposeful touch for the rest of my life. Like this sapling, green and tender, I would bend and turn under His hand until someday I, too, would reach maturity, a woman after His own heart, carefully trained in the direction of His perfect will.

Now, years later, that "someday" had evolved into today, but not with the noble outcome I had envisaged, for that young girl had not grown into a woman after His own heart. The very thing I had feared as a child, and then had learned not to fear as a new Christian, had come upon me in spite of it all. *Tragically, I had missed the purpose.* And since full-grown gnarled trees can't be ungnarled, I felt stuck with myself as I was. In moments of despondency I thought of people without Christ in their lives, and strangely, I envied them. Their lives at least held the possibility of receiving good news, and it seemed mine didn't. Held out to them was the supreme offer of knowing Christ personally and receiving eternal life. But I already had met Christ in this profound way at my conversion. I felt ashamed to wish for more good news than this. Obviously I was a failure as a Christian, merely a "saved sinner" rather than a lost one.

One morning after all these ponderings, I stopped what I was doing, walked over to where my sorely neglected Bible lay, and sat down to read. I had no idea at the time what prompted me to do so, except for a quiet inner stirring that made me *want* to. Simple as that. Within moments it became clear that it was the Spirit of God hovering over me, seeking to bring order at last out of chaos. As I casually picked up my Bible, it fell open by itself to the writings of Jeremiah the prophet, chapter 18, and I began to read. In my imagination I accompanied Jeremiah, who was being sent down to the potter's workshop. God had told him to go, observe the potter at work, and then receive a message to pass on to the wayward people of Israel. As I read along, I felt as if I were peering over Jeremiah's shoulder as he watched the potter working a lump of clay on his wheel. I began to get quite emotionally involved when I read that the clay became marred in the potter's hand. Jumping ahead of the story in my thinking, I assumed that the potter in dismay would toss aside the lump of spoiled clay and take up another, hoping for better results. For a moment, my life was that spoiled lump of clay, and attached to it was the same old nagging fear that God, like this potter, might lay aside my disappointing life and take up another to do His work. But my confused outlook was clarified as I read on to see what the potter really did with the clay: ". . . so he made it over, *reworking it* into another vessel, as it seemed good to the potter to make it" (Jer. 18:4 AMPLIFIED, emphasis mine).

Wait a minute, I cautioned myself against a new surge of hope, *how can I be sure that this story is meant to be applied to my life in the way I would wish?* As if the passage were written for me alone instead of for Israel, it gave me the answer from the Lord in the next two verses, 5 and 6: "Then the word of the LORD came to *me:* '. . . can I not do with you as this potter does?' declares the LORD. 'Like clay in the hand of the potter, so *are you* in my hand' " (NIV, emphasis mine).

At long last, through His Spirit at work within me, God was daring me to believe once and for all what seemed almost too good to believe: contrary to my own merciless, graceless thinking, He did not despise me for my condition. He in fact loved me enough to want me just as I was, with nothing to offer Him but the marred clay of my life. To Him, this lump of clay was not going to be grounds for putting my life on the shelf. Instead, it would be grounds for changing me and healing me to help others. No longer did I need to envy good news for lost sinners. I now had good news of my own, good news for saved sinners like me, and it was this:

> God does not see our messed up lives as gnarled trees; He sees us as marred clay. *And marred clay in the Potter's hand can be refashioned,* as seems *good* to the Potter to make it.

Sanity in the Supermarket

3 I had heard it said that the sweetest sound in all the world is the sound of one's own name. But at this point, almost from one day to the next, I found myself being attracted to a word that excited me far more than my own name, and that word was "*change.*" Whenever I came across it in headlines, in magazines, in advertising, it was a thrilling reminder of the secret between God and me, that I *could* be changed and *would* be changed, beginning now.

As far as I was concerned, one of the most obvious areas in which I needed to experience change was this state of creeping insanity that would come upon me every time I entered a supermarket. *I must be the only person in the whole world suffering like this,* I often thought in my ignorance. And what acute suffering it was.

I really couldn't remember when it all started. All I knew was that this mysterious emotional disturbance was taking me over and I felt powerless to do anything but give in to it. I had gotten to the place where I would have preferred having all my teeth pulled to going to the supermarket. So I'd delay my shopping for as long as I could. I was amazed how resourceful I could be, making something reasonably healthy and interesting from leftover bits of this and that found in the cupboard or refrigerator. But eventually the day of reckoning would come. Nothing to eat—this was the stark reality that would finally make necessity stronger than fear.

Off I'd go to the supermarket, determined to get it over and done with at whirlwind speed and rush back home where I knew a wave of relief would be waiting for me just inside my door. *Remember, it's only up the road,* I'd reassure myself as I walked along, already starting to feel exposed and vulnerable. *And anyway, I need only a few things. Maybe this time it won't be so bad.* But as soon as I'd pass through the automatic door and hear it close behind me, the palms of my hands would begin to drip with nervous sweat. Pushing a shopping cart with one hand and gripping a shopping list with the other, my tense eyes would search for this item and that. The act of looking up and down the shelves, searching and selecting from so many options, would bring on a dizziness behind my eyes that made me feel faint. Before long, rising fear and panic would spread throughout my being; my pulse would begin to pound in my chest and my head until I'd feel that at any moment I might be carried over the cliff-edge of sanity. Sometimes I'd manage to get a handful of groceries to the check-out aisle and paid for before making the mad dash for home. Other times, I'd shove the cart against a wall and hurry home empty-handed only to return later to go through the whole painful process again.

Yes, this was definitely a problem that God was going to have to tackle. Of course, I still had no idea that my complaint was a common one and that it went by the name of agoraphobia. But one thing was becoming clear: God was intending to do far more than a reform job on me. Until recently, all I had wanted was to *feel* better so that I could get on with life as I believed I should be living it. But I had been wanting the end without the means. God was now showing me that the only means for *feeling* more sane was to start *thinking* more sanely—in other words, to start thinking as *He* thought, with heart, mind, soul, and strength.

My Jeremiah experience had been a small but significant start in that direction. Through God's message of refashioned clay, I had been reminded of something I had lost sight of—that His grace and forgiveness is for Christians too! From then on the whole point of His dealings with me would not be condemnation, as I had wrongly thought. It would be *change*—change in my thinking, change in my actions and my reactions. Then, as a result (at least I was daring to hope for this), the healing of my overwhelming emotional symptoms would come.

In all of this I was becoming a student again, the Lord's student. And like any good teacher, He considered it no waste of time to take His student back to basics as a starting point. Without delay, in fact close on the heels of my Jeremiah experience, the Holy Spirit gave me my first assignment by impressing four elementary words on my mind: *read, pray, trust, and obey.* As these four words were brought to my attention, I knew He was asking me, *"Are these four commands really so hard for you? Won't you now, at long last, finally do what I ask?"*

At the imploring tone of His questions I felt sorrow, the sort of soul-ache that comes when you're reminded how very much and how very long you've grieved someone you love. A few lines in Jeremiah 2:32 came back to me: "Does a maiden forget her jewelry, a bride her wedding ornaments? Yet my people have forgotten me, days without number" (NIV). *Days without number.* That was the statistical truth of my spiritual neglect. And yet now, for the first time ever, I felt able to face the pain of my failure. Amazingly enough, the very One I had neglected was now helping me establish a new, improved track record, not as an atonement for the old track record that had failed Him so miserably (His death on the cross had atoned for that), but as the beginning of a brand new thing in my life. I didn't know yet what to call this "new thing," but one day, not too far up the road, I would pinpoint this four-fold discipline as its launching pad.

In his book *Celebration of Discipline,* Richard Foster writes, "God has given us the Disciplines of the spiritual life as a means of receiving His grace. It is 'grace' because it is free; it is 'disciplined' because there is *something for us to do"* (emphasis mine).

These four disciplines were indeed something for me to do. On a daily basis I was to begin fulfilling those spiritual responsibilities that I had neglected for so long. I'm glad to say that I no longer felt pressured to fulfill them simply because this is what Christians are supposed to do. At last I understood, *really* understood, that these four disciplines were every bit as vital to my spiritual health as eating, breathing, sleeping, and exercising are to my physical health. With no further delay, that very day I began reading, praying, trusting, and obeying on a daily basis.

Bill was still in Norway of course; Christina (now fondly called Tina) was at school, and Heidi was in a local playgroup. My aloneness, once seen as a negative element in my life, now turned into a positive opportunity to reestablish my personal Christian life. Pulling an inexpensive paperback copy of the New Testament out of the bookcase and grabbing a ballpoint pen, I settled myself comfortably in my favorite chair (a rocking chair!) and enjoyed the first of many daily "coffee breaks" with the Lord, as I came to call them. That day the Bible ceased being the dust and guilt collector it once was. Little by little this book, rather than me, would become the one that was falling apart at the seams. As a volume, it would be well broken-in by all the handling, underlining, marking, and circling of old and new insights found along the way.

As a start in my discipline of reading, I decided to go back to the four gospels—Matthew, Mark, Luke, and John. I wanted to rediscover more of what Jesus really was like and what He really had taught. Although this was familiar territory for me, page by page I found a composite picture of a more authentic Jesus coming into view. *How surprising!* I thought to myself one day. *The Jesus I'm reading about today seems much more compassionate, much more "the helper of the helpless" than I remembered Him being!* These daily discoveries, made through reading my Bible, provided a natural bridge into the second discipline—praying.

Each day after absorbing a digestible amount of gospel material and with my eyes still open in order to follow along the flow of my underlining and markings, I would begin praying by saying back to God all the things I believed He had said to me from His Word. *This must be what people mean when they talk about dialogue in prayer,* I concluded enthusiastically. And what good company the Lord was as I acknowledged gems of revealed truth, talked over with Him their meaning and application, sat back in silence to meditate or rest in His presence, claimed for myself blessings and promises discovered along the way, thought through any commands or forms of direction as they arose, and bent my will to repent whenever needed, especially concerning my established habit of coming to God as a last resort rather than as a first. This habit, He had shown me, was spiritual rebellion. Until then, rebellion was a word I had used to describe delinquent young people, not me, delinquent though I myself had been!

As far as the discipline of trust was concerned, it seemed clear that in all matters beyond my control (that included every one of my distressing psychological symptoms as well as my acute sense of inadequacy), I had only two choices: to fret over them (a well-practiced skill of mine) or to roll them at last onto His strong shoulders with the admission *I've carried these unbearable burdens too long, Lord, so you'll have to carry them from now on. If there's anything you want me to know or do, I wait for you to show this to me. In the meantime, these problems are* yours, not mine!

And finally I took on the responsibility of obedience. Day by day I sought to view obedience in the light of 1 John 5:3: "This is love for God: to obey his commands. And his commands are not burdensome" (NIV). This verse seemed to split the word responsibility right down the middle— *response* and *ability.* The words "love for God" reminded me that obedience is not a mere duty, it should be our loving response to the God who loved us first. And the words, "his commands are not burdensome," reminded me that His commands will never be greater than my ability to obey them if only I am willing. I began to commit myself to a life of loving and willing obedience—no excuses allowed, only repentance!

I still had a long way to go, but at least I was on the trip back up. "Lift-off" had taken place through these four basic disciplines, and in turn they were giving the Lord more and more access to the clay of my life. Richard Foster, commenting further on the pathway of discipline, writes: "This path leads to the inner transformation and healing for which we seek. We must always remember that *the path does not produce the change; it only puts us in the place where the change can occur."* These four disciplines, I knew, were putting me in that place of change.

"Why on earth didn't I start doing this long ago?" I sighed to the Lord after one of our exceptional coffee breaks. As quickly as I had said it, I was given a clear understanding of the answer. First of all, during our years in Berlin I honestly thought that my spiritual negligence was rooted in lack of time. But now in Geneva there had been plenty of time and still I hadn't read or prayed with any regularity. No, the problem wasn't a matter of time, it was a matter of the will, an unyielded will.

But I also saw there was more to it than the question of my will. Something else had crept in to dampen my smoldering devotional life, nearly snuffing it out completely, and that something else was guilt. As I now saw it, this guilt was like a coin, having two sides to it. One side was *real guilt* (that is, my unyielded will), but the flip side was *false guilt.* From somewhere I had gotten the idea that there was an unwritten but binding spiritual *law,* a law I often broke, that requires Christians to study the Bible and intercede in prayer *before breakfast* seven days a week regardless of circumstances. Looking back, I probably drew this conclusion from a strain of dogmatic Bible teaching that emphasized those occasions when Jesus got up long before dawn and prayed (as in Mark 1:35) and that legalistically imposed these examples as our sole model for personal prayer. It was a worthy model, of course, but hardly carved in granite and certainly not the eleventh commandment, not even in the life of Jesus Himself, I later discovered!

The real damper, however, was a second unwritten law that warned me that if I broke the first law—the law of before-breakfast prayer—then a choice to read and pray *after* breakfast was spiritual compromise, an act of giving God second best. As I couldn't bear to give God second best, reading and praying after breakfast seemed pointless. And so, as time went on, prayer gradually was omitted altogether. Month after month, year upon year, this ridiculous but tortuous false guilt dominated much of my devotional life.

Now, however, I had been set free of both guilts, the real and the false, and I was beginning to function in that freedom. On a daily basis I was doing the right things for the right reasons at last, learning to be cooperative clay in the Potter's hand. Just ahead of me lay the moment for which I had waited so long—my first experience of being "healed in such a way" that similar healing might be available to others.

Not surprisingly, that first healing had its beginning in one of my spiritual coffee breaks. As I sat reveling in the written Word, the still, small voice of the Lord spoke a thought into my mind. *"My Word is full of truth that works,"* was the thought. That was all. *I believe that, Lord,* I answered simply, not sure where He was taking me. *Please put it to work in my life, for any truth that's not working in me is not my truth!* Once more the Lord was showing Himself to be the great prayer-giver, and, as always, He could be counted on to answer the prayer He had given.

At the end of our coffee break, I went into the kitchen, opened my cupboards, and like old Mother Hubbard, found that my cupboards were bare. I could postpone my visit to the supermarket no longer. As on many previous occasions, I was face to face with my emotional aversion to shopping; yet again I was minutes away from a repeat performance of getting part way through my shopping and being overtaken by a wave of panic and perspiration. Today, however, I sensed that I was face to face with a test, not only a test of me myself, but also of God's Word. In the face of such a test, I was counting on some truth that works!

I sank down in my rocking chair and sat for a long moment in the Lord's presence. As I reviewed my intention to trust Him fully for my unbearable shopping problem, I prayed my usual prayer: *If there's anything you want me to know or do, Lord, please show me, for this is still your problem, not mine!*

In that moment I understood quite plainly what He wanted me to do. There was nothing extraordinary about it. I was simply to go out and do my shopping, but this time with a difference. This time, instead of reacting in one of my old ways, which always meant avoiding, postponing, or running away from the panic, I was to carry out my shopping and complete it even if it killed me, making *Him* responsible for whatever happened, whether good or bad.

"All right, Lord, I'm going shopping," I announced at last, "and for all I know it may turn out to be the same old story—the usual panic and perspiration, the usual fear of sudden insanity, and most of all the fear of collapsing wild-eyed on the floor in front of other shoppers and hearing them exclaim 'Whatever's the matter with *her*?' And who knows? The things I fear really could happen. But, Lord, if they do happen, even this is going to be your problem, not mine!"

I prayed it sincerely, not cynically, for I had said it in the faith that this was the proposition for which He had been preparing me. Indeed, it was a pattern I had seen working throughout the gospels: *God longs for the opportunity to be actively and thoroughly responsible for us.* Of course, it was one thing to acknowledge this principle devotionally at home in my rocking chair, but the question was this: Would that same principle prove to be a workable truth for me out there in the maddening aisles of the supermarket—today, next week, next month? And would it lead to my healing?

There was only one way to find out. Off I went with clammy hands to the corner supermarket. Up and down the aisles I moved, making haste as slowly as I could. Though I felt a rising panic, I carried on, for I was going for broke! *If I end up on the floor, so what?* I found myself thinking with an abandonment I had never felt before. Though I earnestly hoped that it wouldn't happen, for the first time it seemed oddly all right if it did. *I'll just lie there and wait for whomever or whatever the Lord sends,* I resolved as I mechanically filled my shopping cart, *for that's His responsibility. Mine is to get the shopping done!*

Finally I reached the cash register, paid for my goods, received change with the usual "merci beaucoup," and headed for home. Once there I flung myself tired but triumphant into my rocking chair. Rocking myself back to stability, I weighed things up in my mind. What was it that had given me the courage, the sheer *guts,* to do the thing I dreaded and to follow it through? I knew exactly what it had been. Those redefined lines of responsibility held the key: *while I was looking after the shopping, I was trusting the Lord to look after me!* I had gone to the supermarket utterly committed to that arrangement.

Shopping days came and went, and it is enough to say that I never, ever postponed shopping or ran out of the supermarket again, though I'll confess I often felt like it. What enabled me not to do it then? By now my long-range goal of *eventual* inner wholeness dominated my actions more than my *immediate* drive to feel good. The relief of feeling good would come as a later benefit, of that I was sure, but it must not be taken as a starting point.

In the meantime, because my source was God rather than myself and because I could depend on Him to be responsible not only for me personally but for every eventuality concerning me, whether good or bad, I was able to do all needful things, even painful things, "through Christ who strengthens me" (Phil. 4:13). In fact, I eventually got used to the pain and learned that I needn't give in to it, that it wouldn't *damage* me to do the things I dreaded.

On that basis I got to the supermarket and back home again time after time, still sane and with my groceries in hand, bags of them! As far as this problem was concerned, I was on my way to wholeness and I knew it. Very slowly I was beginning to feel better too. God had begun to heal me "in such a way," and that way involved learning to operate in dependence on Him.

The Grand Canyon of Bitterness

4 *But Lord, I feel I've got a right to be bitter!*
Self-justifying though it was, this was my frank
response as I sensed the Holy Spirit laying His
finger on my bitterness problem, letting me
know that this was the next item on His healing
agenda.

I had brought this confrontation on myself a few
minutes earlier when I had prayed: "Lord, what's the matter
with *me*?" I knew what was wrong with everybody else, or so
I had thought, plus I had prided myself on never being
resentful unjustifiably. Mine was always a just cause! But
now a true humbling was taking place, a new attitude that
put a familiar tune on my lips as I went around the house
dusting the furniture: "It's *me*, it's *me*, it's *me*, O Lord,
standing in the need of prayer; not my brother, not my sister,
but it's *me*, O Lord, standing in the need of prayer!"

And yet, once the dusting was done I was overtaken
by my usual compulsion to sit down and start polishing my
"bitterness habit." Sad to say, it had become a daily routine
of mine, petting my pet peeves, grieving over my grievances,
and brooding over my hurts one by one. But the price was
high, for I was beginning to resemble Frederick Buechner's
description of the anger found in bitterness: "Of the seven
Deadly Sins, anger is possibly the most fun. To lick your
wounds, to smack your lips over grievances long past, to
savor to the last toothsome morsel both the pain you are
given and the pain you are giving back—in many ways it is a
feast fit for a king. The chief drawback is that what you are
wolfing down is yourself. *The skeleton at the feast is you!*"

For a very long time I had been indulging myself in that "sick fun," and here I was doing it again. But this time, like the day God had stopped me cutting my "life hymn" out of my Bible, He broke into my unwholesome brooding with a fatherlike rebuke in my heart: *"That's* what's wrong with you—*bitterness!"* Except for that rebuke and His counsel that followed, my life eventually might have self-destructed in some serious way. As it was, I already had a big black hole inside me that seemed nearly the size of the Grand Canyon, carved out little by little by all my negative emotions and slowly being filled up with my accumulating unhappiness.

The Lord's timing in tackling my bitterness problem was impeccable, for Bill was still on that long, nine-week visit to Norway, touring with a select group of American students called a "Teen Team." As their appointed team leader, Bill's demanding role was to bring strong oversight to their lives and ministry as they went from school to school, communicating the gospel with a very high standard of music and witness. Neither Bill nor I had an inkling of the Lord's hidden agenda to change *both* of us at exactly the same time.

Meanwhile, "back at the ranch" in Geneva, the Lord was wasting no time getting to the heart of my bitterness problem, for there was no time to waste. In response to my words, "I feel I've got a right to be bitter," the Lord dropped these solemn words into my mind: *"That may be, but as long as you cling to that right, you will remain unwhole."* Immediately I felt Him distance Himself from me just as described in Hosea 5:15, "I will go back to my place until they admit their guilt. And they will seek my face; in their misery they will earnestly seek me" (NIV).

I was sobered but not alarmed by the space between us, for I understood that I was being left with a choice that was mine to make, a far-reaching, fateful choice. Which was it going to be then? Would I cling to my so-called right to bitterness and slowly eat myself alive? Or would I give up my sense of being right and move further into wholeness instead? Surely it should have been an easy decision, considering my options. But it wasn't.

My immediate decision, of course, was to give up my bitterness. Any way I looked at it, this was the right thing to do. As soon as I had made that rational decision, however, my clamoring emotions forced me to unmake it. Tied up with my bitterness habit was a certain sort of comfort: someone understood, even if that someone was only me! This, I knew, was the pathetic brand of comfort I was deriving from my daily "pity party." How could I bear to give up that security blanket of self-comfort, for it seemed the only real solace I had.

One or two days passed. I was sick of my indecision, sick of keeping the Lord waiting. Finally I began to think in terms of that purpose that I had nearly missed, and that still could be missed unless I got this issue right. At life's end, how could I possibly argue that my bitterness had been justifiable grounds for missing my destiny in Christ? In any case, wasn't this bitterness habit part of the marred clay He was waiting to refashion, a very big part?

Back into my rocking chair I got, ready to do business with God. In an earnest tone I spoke aloud, "All right, Lord, I've made my decision." Instantly I sensed His presence drawing near again, waiting to hear the words He doubtless already knew, but words He wanted *me* to declare. "I've chosen not to cling to my rights any longer, Lord. I'm choosing wholeness instead of bitterness, not simply for my sake, but also for your sake, so that you'll be honored through your purpose in my life. But there's one big problem, Lord . . ." I went on, almost as if this one were going to stump even Him, ". . . *how* do I stop being bitter?"

A big problem? To whom? It soon became clear that it was baffling only to me, certainly not to the Lord! Under these circumstances not even my faith (or lack of it) seemed to be a major issue, but rather my willingness. My question, "How can I stop?" had been understood by the Lord as a willingness to learn.

What transpired after that can be explained only in terms of the Holy Spirit's ministry as our *divine Counselor.* In the Gospels Jesus referred to Him several times as the "other Counselor," the Spirit of Christ Himself who would come to take up office within us. From that inner sanctuary Jesus said that the Spirit would activate His counseling ministry by teaching us and reminding us of the truth, by giving us a clear testimony of Christ, by convicting and guiding us, and finally by drawing from *the things that are Christ's* and disclosing them to us (John 16:14 AMPLIFIED).

The Holy Spirit now began to minister Christ's counsel and wisdom to me in the form of *inner instructions,* seven progressive steps of deliverance from bitterness. These steps were not invented by me but were impressed on my mind by the Holy Spirit, *one step at a time.* How He communicated these to me, I'll never be able to prove, but I'm assured that I'm not alone in this mystery. In fact, it encourages me no end that even the apostle Paul could get no further explaining the "mechanics" of his revelations than to say twice, "I do not know—God knows."(2 Cor. 12:2-3 NIV). What Paul *did* know and boldly taught in 1 Corinthians 2:16 was this: anyone attempting to instruct the Lord is attempting the impossible, but if we long for *Him* to instruct us, then, mysterious as it is, the Holy Spirit is there to make that possible, even giving us "words taught by the Spirit, expressing spiritual truths in spiritual words." Paul called it having the mind of Christ (1 Cor. 2:13, 16).

Step one came across as rather elementary at first. I was to make a list of all the people and situations over which I felt angry, bitter, or hateful. *Oh sure,* I thought to myself as I took pen and paper, *I'm familiar with this idea. We had to do this sort of thing as kids at church camp, tossing our lists* *into the campfire on the closing night.* I was already trying to think of a suitable place to build a private bonfire, should this be what the Lord had in mind.

With pen and paper in hand and without a second thought, I wrote Bill's name at the top of my paper. Then I stopped, choking up inside. This was going to be a lot more painful than my youth camp experience had been. I could see it all clearly: making this list was going to be like unbolting the door of my emotions, swinging it wide open, and watching my painful feelings march through that open door and line up in front of me. It didn't occur to me that this was the whole point of the exercise. For a start I felt downright guilty seeing Bill's name at the top of my list, for we loved each other deeply, with a love strong as death. And yet it was the very strength of our love that made me so dissatisfied with things as they were. My chief complaint was a common one. Bill took so little time for me and the girls, so little time just to laugh or make small-talk with us. He gave little more than a passing glance at the odd-shaped "works of art" the girls created just for him in his absence and presented to him with such excitement. At mealtimes his thoughts were anywhere but on the food he was eating and who he was eating it with. So fully absorbed was his mind in weightier matters that one had to break into his concentration just to ask for the salt. Whether at home or away, our beloved hubby and daddy simply wasn't with us, and we were missing him desperately.

So long as we lived in Berlin, of course, Bill and I were working side by side, rather like Siamese twins, as I've already said. Unfortunately our lives centered entirely on work and little else, but at least we were working together. Now that Bill was traveling, however, I hardly knew who I was apart from him. Every time he left on another journey, I felt as if my own identity had been shut into his suitcase and had been carried away with him. At home there seemed little left of myself but a rather useless, empty shell, waiting for my husband and my identity to come back to me.

I wanted to close the door against any further emotions pouring out, but it was too late. The deepest ones were already out, with many smaller ones clamoring to follow suit. My only comfort was this—the Lord had ordered it. That being the case, I decided to go whole hog and ensure that nothing got left behind. *Help me to remember everything, Lord. Don't let me stop until it's all out.* I was beginning to get the right idea. I moved on down the page, adding name after name, event after event, injury after injury, some going back rather a long time, some only going back to the previous week. I laid the paper down and gave it a rest. I went to bed, got up, and came back to it the next day. Finally I knew there was nothing more. It was out—all of it!

Then **step two** became clear: in God's presence I was to go through the list person by person and say, "I forgive so-and-so for doing or saying such-and-such or for *not* doing or saying such-and-such!" Through the Spirit I was made to understand that the essence of this step was *action rather than emotion.* I was being asked simply to *do* it, nothing more. As I forgave each one, I too claimed much-needed forgiveness for my bitter reaction to these offenses. It took rather a long time and not a few tears to get through it all. My emotions were a mixed bag, but I continually reminded myself that it was my obedience that counted at this point.

Step three came quickly on the heels of step two, but it still wasn't bonfire time yet! No, I was to go through the list yet again (by now it was nearly memorized) and release each person, not into thin air, but rather *to God* saying, "I release so-and-so to you, Lord. You alone know if this person needs changing, and if so, you alone can do it." In my sanctified imagination, each person, once a heavy boulder in my heart, became instead like a big rubber ball held in both my hands and thrown into God's hands by my prayer of release. With each ball, I visualized God reaching out, catching it, and taking it safely into His care. What a vast collection of rubber balls He accumulated that day! And what a great number of boulders were excavated out of my Grand Canyon of bitterness!

Now a bonfire, Lord? By no means, for in **step four** He had me going through the list yet again, this time praying *for,* rather than *against* each person. In other words, I was not to say, "Oh Lord, please help so-and-so not to be such a so-and-so!" Instead I was to pray positively for them by saying things like, "Please bless and encourage this person, enter into every need and problem, bring to this person your strength, hope, and victory." Somewhere along the line as I prayed in this manner, a tiny flame was lit in that black hole within me. I had a feeling that this flame, timid and tiny as it was, would be igniting the only bonfire the Lord wanted me to have—not a bonfire on some lone beach, but a bonfire within my inner Grand Canyon, not a bonfire to consume a written record of bitterness, but a bonfire to consume the bitterness itself, root and all.

That night I went to bed and slept soundly, wrapped in a blanket of peace rather than self-pity. The next morning I got up wondering, *What if bitter feelings return? What would the Lord want me to do in such a case?* His answer came to me in **step five:** now that I had released each person to God, if an attitude of bitterness or anger were to arise, I was to confess it promptly to God and promptly claim His forgiveness. Then I was to go right on maintaining an attitude of seeing other people *still* in God's hands instead of mine, *still* in His keeping instead of mine, *still* forgiven, and *still* the object of my positive prayers.

Step six was rather exciting, for now I was to start watching for even the slightest sign that God was answering my positive prayers for others, and I was to give Him all the praise. *However*—and this was a very big however—my involvement in prayer was to remain a secret between the Lord and me. He wasn't going to allow me to be proud instead of bitter. I wasn't going to be allowed to go to the other person and say, "I'm so pleased over your obvious spiritual growth. Of course I've been praying for this for some time."

In any case, my occupation (or preoccupation) was no longer focused on the flaws of others. That was God's business. My business, my *only* business, was **step seven:** to depend on God utterly to go on changing the marred clay of my life and through that dependence to be cooperative clay in His hands. Others I could leave safely with Him.

This is almost miraculous! I rejoiced as I reflected on the week just past. *One day I'm telling the Lord I have a right to be bitter; a few days later I'm praising Him for helping me kick the bitterness habit!* I knew that I was still capable of being bitter, but *I wasn't bitter now,* and I need never be bitter again, except for the few minutes it would take to go through those seven steps again if necessary. The Holy Spirit not only had shown me how to stop being bitter, *He had taught me what to do instead of being bitter.* The divine Counselor had taken the things that were Christ's—wisdom, understanding, knowledge, and the fear of the Lord—and had disclosed them to me. And as part of the package, He again was getting more of my thinking straight.

For example, there was a time when I felt that Jesus had been extremely harsh in Matthew 5:21-22 when He said that anger and murder deserved exactly the same judgment. Now through the eyes of my Counselor I saw that anger is indeed the *seed* of murder; that the final outgrowth of that seed, if allowed to develop to its ultimate extent, would become the *deed* of murder. Therefore, persistent anger with all its bitterness, in some tragic sense, is *slow murder toward others* and *slow suicide toward ourselves*—very unhealthy for all involved.

I also understood that, humanly speaking, bitterness is the natural thing unless we discover something better. There is a legalistic fairness and logic to it that our carnal natures love, like the "eye for an eye, and tooth for a tooth" principle that Jesus referred to in His famous Sermon on the Mount. But in that same sermon Jesus calls us away from the natural thing, away from the fair and logical thing. Instead He calls us to live a supernatural life through Him, which in turn sets us free to live as He lived: to reconcile ourselves to others, to turn the other cheek, to go the extra mile, to love our so-called enemies, and to *pray for them!* All in all we're to become perfectly whole and complete *in spirit,* even as our heavenly Father is perfect.

With my growing sense of sanity in the supermarket and my increasing love for others, plus beginning to feel better, I was getting eager for Bill's return. What a lot had transpired during his absence. Would he notice that he had come home to a better wife than he left nine weeks earlier? Little did I know that there was as much surprise in store for me as for Bill.

Finally the day of his return had come. It was a long day for all of us for he wouldn't be arriving until late evening. As I tucked Tina and Heidi in bed, they were giggly and excitable, almost like on the night before Christmas. After their prayers they would shut their eyes tightly and fall asleep quickly, letting the oblivion of sleep hasten the morning when they would wake up at the crack of dawn to look for signs that Daddy was home: suitcases in the hall, a coat thrown over a chair, tired looking shoes tossed to one side, car keys and loose change on the coffee table. Although not yet seeing or touching him in the flesh, they would race back to their beds more than satisfied that their warm, strong Daddy was home at last!

I turned off their light and went into the living room to continue waiting for his arrival and to listen for the familiar sound of our Opel station wagon pulling into the parking area below. I had changed into something feminine and pink— Bill's favorite color on me. I decided not to rush down on the elevator to meet him when I heard him come. No, I would let him come up, let himself into the apartment, and find me seated alluringly on the sofa in our dimly lit living room, ready and waiting to be taken into his arms and held.

As I waited, I prayed for his safety and I prayed for "us." At last I heard the sound of an Opel down below coming to a stop, the sound of heavy things being unloaded, the sound of the elevator traveling downwards, pausing at ground-floor level, and then traveling up again and stopping at our floor. My heart leapt at the sound of luggage being slid from the elevator to our doorstep and the fumbling of a key being inserted and turned in the lock. Perhaps I should run to greet him, to help him, I thought. But no, he too wanted it this way, I felt. Finally I heard the bags being shoved into our hall and the door being closed quietly behind him. A few more heavy footsteps and then he appeared around the corner, all six foot three of him, and oh so handsome there in the shadows. He paused a moment, then rushed to my side on the couch. A long, warm kiss and embrace were exchanged, and then something touching happened, something almost alarming.

Bill lowered his head into my lap and began to sob quietly, his shoulders and hands tense with emotion. Bill wasn't one to cry, so it was important that I not be too quick to question him. Had he had an accident with the car, I wondered inwardly? Bill hardly would have let something like that throw him, especially since he obviously was safe and sound. Whatever could have happened to so crush my never-say-die, gotta-keep-moving husband? Shortly he regained his composure. Sitting up and giving a sigh of emotional relief, he began to tell me what it was all about.

"You know, Joanie," he began, "I felt so challenged being appointed Teen Team leader. On my way up to Norway I committed myself to being the best team leader the group could have. I was going to be 'big Daddy' to those kids. I was going to anticipate their every need, be aware of their hopes and dreams, have fun with them, listen to them. Every day I made sure I carried out my commitment. Sometimes it was really tough, and yet it was so fulfilling."

Bill started to choke up again but quickly recovered to continue, "And then I started feeling uneasy inside myself. Day after day I felt it, but I couldn't figure out what it was. Finally I prayed about it, and then I saw it clearly," he said tearfully. "All the things I was trying to be to this team were the very things I hadn't begun to be to you and the girls." Taking me in his arms, Bill went on to say, "Up there in Norway I made another commitment, that by God's grace I was going to be all of these things to my own family. And I couldn't wait to get home to tell you!"

Now we were both sobbing. I hardly knew what to say, but one thing I *didn't* say was, "You'll be interested to know, dear, that I've been praying for a long time for this!" Oh no, I only nestled in his arms and purred my praise to that great Counselor who had done vastly more than answer prayer. He had moved a huge roadblock out of His way by removing my bitterness, for now I knew that *bitterness blocks God!* Once the blockage was gone, once I had released Bill to God and had made it my business to depend on Him to change and control *me,* He wasted no time working on both of us—a literal fulfillment of our wedding prayer: "Have Thine own way Lord, have Thine own way; Thou art the Potter, *we* are the clay."

That night in Geneva, Switzerland, the biggest bonfire ever was ignited and flared up in a certain displaced Grand Canyon. Only the angels in heaven could see it, and I dare say they were having a party!

The Embarrassment of God-Dependence

5 By now I was beginning to notice a paradox at work in my growing wholeness. Absurd as it sounds, whenever I was confronted by my frustrating weakness, which was still rather often, I had to admit that the key to overcoming it was weakness itself.

Catherine Marshall made the same absurd point in her well-loved book *Beyond Ourselves.* "Helplessness," she wrote, "is actually one of the greatest assets a human being can have." And then, no doubt realizing how much her words would offend our deeply ingrained self-sufficiency, she went on to explain that crisis has a way of bringing us face to face with our inadequacy, so that our inadequacy in turn can lead us to the inexhaustible sufficiency of God. "This" she insisted, "is the power of helplessness, a principle written into the fabric of life."

The more I experienced this strange power of helplessness and weakness, the more its principle was being inscribed into the fabric of my own life. Ingrained still deeper, however, was another principle—an ever-so-decent streak of independence that gave me the fear of using God like a crutch. In fact, the very thought of such a possibility caused me uncomfortable feelings of embarrassment.

In the meantime I had learned to drive. No one but God and I knew how costly those driving lessons had been, not in terms of money but in terms of nerve-racking effort. However, the moment I had passed my test, Bill expected me to be prepared to drive anywhere and everywhere, bless him, and he gave me ample responsibilities that forced me to do exactly that. In time I became a good driver, but initially, the fear of going where I'd never been, of getting lost and not knowing what to do, of dangerous driving conditions and accidents—things that most other drivers take in their stride—were monumental undertakings that were even more nerve-racking than learning to drive in the first place.

One day when the simple task of driving from A to B turned into another one of my grand achievements through reliance on God, I became aware of an underlying tension in my outlook. Pulling me in one direction was this gut-level embarrassment about all-out dependence on God, although, as yet, I stood little chance of managing without the dependence. Pulling me from the other side, however, was the sheer sense of rightness I always experienced in its operation. That day my inner tug-of-war erupted in a jovial, yet serious outburst to God: "I really must look pathetic, Lord!" And glancing heavenward with a sheepish smile I said in jest, "I can almost see the angels shaking their heads in pity as they watch me depend on you for things that most people do like rolling off a log."

There was no doubt about it, a life of such total dependence as this was beginning to have an embarrassing side to it. Wasn't it a bit immature, I asked myself, even downright wrong, for an adult, especially a Christian, to go on depending on anything or on anyone that much, even if that someone is God? I was profoundly grateful, of course, to see my disabled spiritual and emotional life being healed so steadily through the therapy of God-dependence. After all, hadn't I earnestly prayed at rock-bottom level to be "healed in such a way" that one day I could offer similar healing to others like myself? And hadn't the Lord assured me that this was a prayer He intended to answer? Nonetheless, how much longer was this emergency effort going to be needed? This continuous dependence on God as my only reasonable option seemed to place both Him and me in rather unpopular company—that is, in the same negative, neurotic context that commonly surrounds the word *dependence* nowadays.

At this point, one might have expected the Lord to rush in with many convincing proofs to persuade me that depending on Him is far more than a mere rescue operation. But He didn't. He chose instead to bear patiently with my patchy understanding and to let *His* truth become *my* truth through an exciting process of personal experience, a process which He knew lay just before me. Like a developing stage play, the drama of our family life now began to progress quickly from one act to the next, requiring a whole new set of scenery, in fact a whole new location. After thirteen years in Europe, Bill was appointed to become the Overseas Director at our Youth for Christ headquarters in Wheaton, Illinois, which meant that we would be moving back to the U.S., perhaps for several years, perhaps permanently.

Perhaps permanently? Oh God, surely not that! Kneeling alone by our bed I tearfully asked, *What's this move all about, Lord? Is it only about Bill's new appointment and nothing more? Or is it really about me and my failure to pass the missionary test after all, in spite of my recent improvements?* Thirteen years earlier we had left our homeland and had come to Europe on the strength of a clear calling. For me, going back home felt as if we were going back on that call—and all because of me, perhaps. *Oh God,* I pleaded further, *I can't bear to go back unless I know that I, too, am being given something to do, some purpose over there you want me to fulfill.*

I don't know what I expected, or if I expected anything at all. What I got was something too quiet to be proven, even to myself, but far too real to be denied. As I remained bowed at my bedside, a still-life scene was being imposed fleetingly on the walls of my mind. It reminded me of a large snapshot, except different, for I knew it had captured something future rather than something past. My inner eyes were "seeing" a group of women sitting around a large, oval table, each holding and studying a Bible. Though their faces were not distinguishable, two facts were crystal clear: these women were not necessarily practicing Christians, and God was calling me to study the Bible with them.

Launch a Bible study for such as these? I was only aware of committed Christians studying the Bible, for who else would want to? And why should a weakling like me lead the way? A lot of "ifs," "ands," and "buts" began to crowd into my mind. Then I remembered my plea for a purpose only moments before. Though I didn't understand how, the Spirit of God had answered me in no uncertain terms. If I was sincere and if He was God, I was without excuse. If, in God's eyes, my weakness was no obstacle to the fulfillment of His call, what reason was there for my saying no?

All right, Lord . . . I'll do it, I answered out of sheer obedience. *But Lord, it will have to be you doing it through me.* I reached for my Bible and opened to a familiar verse that had slipped into my mind as I prayed: 'The one who calls you is faithful and *he will do it'* (1 Thess. 5:24 NIV, emphasis mine). In the reassuring soil of that promise, I silently planted my tiny mustard seed of faith and left it there, a pact between God and me. Then, without so much as an "Amen," I rose from my knees and mentally began making preparations for our move.

A few hectic months later, within hours, to be exact, of our arrival in West Chicago and taking possession of our new home, we began shopping for new and used furniture, hunting for the best bargains in town. Bill was agreeable and entirely without curiosity when I asked if I might choose the dining-room table. So far I had told no one, not even Bill, of my rather unconvincing Geneva experience. Nonetheless, my unshakable confidence that I would have no problem finding a large, oval table at a reasonable price just like the one in my spiritual "snapshot" let me know that my mustard seed of faith at least had taken root. On our next shopping trip, that faith was not disappointed.

I was at home alone the exciting day that our new table and six matching chairs were delivered. I could hardly take it in. What I was seeing with my eyes and touching with my hands was my own personal experience of faith being turned into sight, of "things hoped for" becoming substance. And all of it, the faith and its fulfillment, was God's doing. Suddenly I had the urge to "sanctify" our table and chairs, to set them apart as sacred items belonging to God for His special use. And so with one hand resting on the table and the other on a chair, I prayed a simple prayer dedicating it all to God. Then the thought came to me, "Why stop there?" With that I went into our kitchen, flung open the cupboard doors where our coffee mugs were stored, and dedicated these too, plus four kitchen chairs, for the service of those who would sit around our table. Lastly I dedicated myself afresh to God, still wondering what had made Him willing to use such frail stuff as I, but believing that this was His plan. I was certain, of course, that He would want me to become much more whole before asking me to make a start. In any case, I didn't yet know any of my neighbors.

Finding no reasonable shortcut for solving that problem, I decided to link myself up with those living around us simply by praying for them. And so it was that each morning, after seeing Tina and Heidi off to school and Bill off to his Wheaton office, I would take a position standing at our large front window as if only enjoying a casual glance up and down the road. Moving my eyes slowly in one direction and then in the other, I would repeat earnestly the same one-sentence prayer of blessing over each house: *Lord, please richly bless the people in the brick house . . . and bless the people in the cream house . . . and bless the people in that odd green house . . .* and on and on, until finally I would wrap it up with . . . *and please bless the people in the houses I can't see from here . . . leave no one out, Lord . . . only bring your love and blessing to* all *the people in* all *the houses in our entire neighborhood!*

Gradually I came to know some of our neighbors and their families by name, which personalized and lengthened my window-side prayers considerably. Soon we were crossing the road for a chat, borrowing the odd cup of sugar or a tool from one another, coming to each other's rescue through small favors, and even planning surprise birthday parties for each other which brought greater togetherness and a bit of celebration to our community life.

One morning Bev, a nearby neighbor of mine, came and dropped herself wearily on one of my kitchen chairs. At first it was just smalltalk. And then, leaning across her cup of coffee as if to speak more confidentially, she shared one family problem after another. As she prepared to leave, I shocked myself as much as Bev by suggesting, "Before you go, Bev, would you mind if I prayed a short prayer about these worrisome things? I personally find a lot of help through prayer."

Bev's color flushed noticeably and so did mine. I quickly bowed my head and squeezed my eyes shut to avoid looking at her as much as to pray and just managed to get through my prayer without breaking out in a nervous rash. With a mumbled "Thank you," Bev went home, leaving me thinking, *I've done it now. She'll never be back!* But she did come back. And so did others, some of whom, I suspect, had heard the latest gossip about their new neighbor who liked to pray for people's problems. A few who came seemed unwilling to leave until a prayer for *their* shared problems had been offered.

At about the same time I was building a friendship with Shirley Brown from our church, a woman as down-to-earth as her name and richly endowed with a love of life and people. In fact, it was Shirley's heart for people that led her to disclose an interesting burden of hers one day as we talked. Of all things, she too longed to get involved in a Bible study with her neighbors, but simply didn't know how to begin. That made two of us! As far as we were concerned, finding this out about each other was a sign that God had been at work in us long before we had met, preparing us and calling us to work together.

Immediately we began to meet for prayer and planning. Our two main concerns were when and how we should take the big plunge. The matter of *when* was made clear to us much sooner than we expected or particularly wanted through one of our pastor's sermons. The Scripture on which he was preaching was from the Old Testament book of Joshua, chapter 1: "So now arise!" God had instructed Joshua. "Every place upon which the sole of your foot shall tread, that I have given to you . . . be strong (confident) and of good courage." In our minds there was no disputing it. This sermon was more than good preaching, it was *God* preaching. His Spirit was using the words of this Scripture to bring direction to Shirley and me just as truly as He had used these same words to direct Joshua. He was telling us that He considered everything and everybody ready for the task *now*—not on some glorious, more secure day in the future, but in the not-so-glorious, somewhat insecure *now*.

Personally, I felt anything but ready. *Lord,* I argued, *you know I'm still so shaky and nervous when under pressure, and besides that, I'm still on tranquilizers. That would hardly be a good witness to those who don't yet know you. What would they think of me, a Christian and a Christian worker, suffering with bad nerves? Surely I must be more whole before taking this on.* But the Lord answered my reasonings by sending an insight out of His own mind and dropping it into mine: *"Unless you do this, you'll not become more whole."* I was beginning, but only just beginning, to understand. Apparently this task was meant not only for the good of others, but for the good of *me*. In exactly what way it was going to be good for me I had no way of knowing, but I could accept it as a reason (it was God's reason, after all) for stepping out in spite of myself.

And so, taking the Lord at His word, Shirley and I agreed that now was the time to begin. With the question of "when" well settled, the question of "how" seemed to answer itself quite naturally as we considered the approaching Easter season. Yes, that was it! We would use "The True Meaning of Easter" as the theme for our first Bible study. Now the only thing left was to step out—literally.

The feelings we experienced as we traipsed from house to house and invited people to come—Shirley in her neighborhood and I in mine—could only be compared to the apprehension one feels when going to the dentist. To be sure, each neighbor listened politely as I delivered my verbal invitation, but not one said whether or not she would come. Still, we had done our part; the rest was out of our hands.

Finally the fateful Wednesday morning arrived. As soon as Bill and the girls were out of the house, I went to work arranging our sanctified chairs around our sanctified table and setting out an assortment of sanctified coffee mugs. In front of each chair I also placed a paperback copy of the New Testament, carefully inserting a bookmark in each one at the selected chapter.

Suddenly a wave of doubt rolled over me to mock me. Who in the world did I think was going to come to this Bible study? Perhaps no one, I admitted frankly to the doubting Thomas within me. But it was too late to back up now. We had gone out on a limb and had sawed it off behind us. God Himself would have to catch and carry us from now on. And if all failed, what then? Was I willing to fail in my efforts for the Lord? I decided then and there that I was.

At that moment of relinquishment I glanced through the window. With disbelief, I saw one neighbor after another making her way gingerly up the street, heading for my house. Among the arrivals were Shirley and several friends from her neighborhood. Soon there were more ladies than sanctified chairs, an exciting dilemma that sent me dragging more chairs out of bedrooms and duly sanctifying them on the way.

Everyone looked ill at ease and nervous, but none more so than I. I was the one person who needed to be oozing with confidence, for it was I who was meant to be in charge! With the coffee supply diminishing and the loud talk escalating, I knew that the dreaded moment had arrived to get everyone's attention and make a start. With all eyes on me I tried to look and sound relaxed, but the piece of paper in my hand and the voice in my throat were trembling conspicuously. I laid the paper down, but I still couldn't disguise my quivering, clammy hands. With a forced, great-to-be-alive smile, I started to give out a warm welcome. Suddenly, mid-sentence, I simply gave up trying to be something I wasn't.

"Ladies," I confessed, looking at them with my first sincere smile of the morning, "I may as well stop pretending that I'm not nervous, because it's obvious that I am. But then, perhaps you're feeling a bit nervous too, not knowing quite what to expect." With that, we all began to smile at each other and relax.

"I may as well warn you," I went on, "that Shirley and I are not a pair of superwomen. To be honest, I've passed through a really tough time recently, and I'm still getting over it. So there is no one here who needs this group more than I do or needs the Lord's strength more than I. In fact, Shirley and I both feel the need to learn more about God, faith, and the Bible, and we decided to invite you, our neighbors, to come along today to join us in this. Thanks for being here this morning. You've encouraged us both. We only hope you'll get some encouragement out of it too."

This was not going according to plan, not at all, and I secretly hoped and prayed that neither God nor Shirley minded too much. Certainly no one else seemed to mind—a passing observation I found rather surprising. If nothing else, honesty and reality had won through.

A number of ladies looked visibly relieved when I invited them to open their Bibles at the bookmark, for it clearly spared anyone the embarrassment of having to flip around in search of the right place. Someone volunteered to read aloud the portion from one of the gospels, which gave us an account of Christ's death and resurrection. Then, with the use of several questions composed by Shirley and me, I began to invite some low-key discussion about the significance of Christ's death for us. *At last things are going as planned!* I sighed inwardly with relief. That is, until Barb, seated at the other end of the table, began to weep. What on earth had we done, or more to the point, what had I done to upset her?

"I'm . . . I'm sorry about this, girls . . ." Barb stammered, choking back tears. As she searched her pockets in vain for something to dry her eyes, I did the practical thing by grabbing a box of tissues and sending it down the table in her direction. Between nose-blows, Barb confessed her fear that her debilitating illness, plus family worries, might be a punishment from God, her "just desserts" for not being a very good mother. Why was everyone suddenly looking at *me?* I opened my mouth and heard myself speak these halting words of gospel truth: "Barb, the Lord isn't punishing you. In fact, He's got good news for you . . . for me . . . for every one of us. When Christ died on the cross—as we've just read—He was actually taking the punishment we all deserve. Instead of punishing us, He's offering us forgiveness—eternal life beginning right now, if only we'll do what you've just done, if only we'll admit our need."

With that another neighbor started to cry. She stretched out her hand for the box of tissues and tearfully began to unburden her own heart. Then several others in turn did the same until the box had been passed up and down the table almost like the elements of Holy Communion. And communion it was indeed, for the living bread of Jesus and the costly wine of His forgiving love were being tasted all around the table—the *Lord's* table. With each burden shared and every tear shed, the real meaning of Easter was being more and more understood and personalized, far beyond our hopes and dreams.

All too soon it was time to bring this sacred hour to a close. But *how,* that was the question. Again, without premeditation on my part, I heard myself making this suggestion: "I'm quite sure that most of us around this table believe in the value of prayer. Since we've opened up and shared so many personal problems that urgently need God's help, shall we close our sharing time by joining hands around the table and praying silently for the person on each side of us? After a short time, I'll bring our prayertime to a close by saying, 'Amen.' "

Silent prayer? Only a puny Amen, nothing more? What a cop-out! I reproached myself inwardly as I watched them bow their heads as one. *I've really messed it up now. A leader is supposed to lead, but now, thanks to my clumsiness, no one is in charge!*

Hands were already reaching out all around the table, tightly gripping someone else's hands, mine included, forming a complete circle. Then came what I fully expected to be an embarrassing, empty silence. But I seemed to be the only embarrassed person there, and the silence was anything but empty. In those quiet moments it became tangibly clear that God's Spirit had come down on our circle and was entering into our unpolished heart-prayers. I too began to pray for my neighbors, silently and fervently.

No one in charge? What an insult to God, for *He* was now in charge, causing us to experience together the reality of

Paul's words in Romans 8:26, "We do not know what we ought to pray for, but the Spirit himself intercedes *for us* with groans that words cannot express" (NIV). I sat amazed and humbled as God used these neighbors of mine to reteach me something I hoped never, ever to forget: the prayer He welcomes is the prayer we were practicing that day—contrite, sincere prayer from the heart. More than ever before in my life, I was now confident that such prayer, with or without words, is heard and understood by God. And not only that, that His Spirit is there to gather up our sighs and tears and translate them into an earnest plea for the will of God in our lives.

After my "Amen," no one made a move to leave but sat basking in the afterglow of what only could be called an encounter with God's love. Finally it was time for me to make this announcement: "When our children are back in school after the Easter break, Shirley and I plan to meet regularly for further study and discussion based on the Bible. Is there anyone here today who would care to join us?"

Outspoken Bev declared her colors then and there by saying, "I don't know about anyone else, but I wish we could do this every day!" From all around the table came other enthusiastic responses. As simple and as profound as that, our Bible study was off the ground.

A few minutes later I was seeing them out the door. As I stood at my prayer window, watching them wend their way home and re-enter their personal worlds, my mind boggled at the tougher, more humbling statement that God was making through these dear hearts and gentle people: that my dependence on Him, a product of my weakness, was no grounds for embarrassment—it had become grounds for a total rethink on my part.

Throughout the rest of the day I kept asking myself the same questions. What exactly was it that lay at the root of my embarrassment over all-out dependence on God? And further, what was my deepest desire as a Christian anyway?

Was it to impress the world with an illusion of *my* greatness or with the reality of *God's* greatness? To my shame, it was clear to me that I had been trying to do both, all in the name of being a "good testimony for Christ." Hence my embarrassment whenever I felt I wasn't the impressive Christian I thought people expected me to be, particularly nowadays when I was being seen and known as a person who *needed* to depend on God.

One fundamental result of my questioning was a renewed longing to impress the world around me with His greatness alone, period. But what quality was He looking for in this earthen vessel of mine, what particular quality would He find most useful in making me a faithful witness of His greatness? This was the central question. When I recalled how impressive God's power and love had been in our midst that morning, I simply couldn't deny the fact that if God had used me at all in this, it had been my weakness and not my strength that He had harnessed; it had been my weakness and not my strength that had given Him free reign to work; it had been my weakness and not my strength that had tapped into His greater strength.

Ah yes, how well acquainted I'd been with the apostle Paul's testimony in 2 Corinthians 12:9-10 in which he speaks of Christ's strength being made perfect in his weakness, a paradox so real in Paul's daily experience that he finally concludes, "when I am weak, then I am strong" (NIV).

Now, at last, I was beginning to know weakness as a true asset, just as Paul did. But more than that, I knew that if Paul's experience was to go on being mine, I would have to be as committed to dependence on God as he obviously was. Unlike me, Paul hadn't minded declaring to the whole world that everything he did was only possible through Christ who strengthened him. If such dependence on God was no embarrassment to the apostle, much less to my West Chicago neighbors, who was I to be embarrassed?

My Neighborhood Experience

6 *All right, Lord . . . what next?* This was the
question now playing on my mind as one day
after another slipped by. There was no doubt
about it, that first unbelievable Bible study was
going to be a hard one to follow, at least from the
human side of things. But follow it we must, for Shirley and I
had promised these hungry lambs, and ourselves, further
nourishment as soon as the Easter holidays were over.

Now more than ever, of course, we were confident that
the Lord was in our midst, waiting to do the works that only
He can do. But what was the Lord counting on us doing? Or
to put it more practically, exactly how were we to conduct all
those Bible studies yet to come? Should we be trying our
own hand at teaching the Bible? The problem was, neither
Shirley nor I felt equipped to take on such a task, much less
to keep it up over many months. In any case, we were
sensing a powerful advantage in being seen and known by
our neighbors simply as their peers rather than as biblical
authorities. If possible, we wanted to keep it that way.

Our best option, we agreed, would be to start looking
for some reliable Bible study materials, prepared and published by experts in this field. But again, how were we to find
what we were looking for, if it indeed existed? Most materials
appeared to be designed mainly for Christians and often
had an approach that assumed a predisposition of faith. We
desperately needed guidance, and we needed it soon.

In his capacity as Overseas Director at Youth for
Christ, Bill came home one evening with an assignment for
me to tackle. I didn't disguise the fact that I wasn't exactly

elated over the prospect of more things to do, preoccupied as I was with this dilemma of "what next" for our Bible study. But there was no passing the buck to anyone else. Apparently it was the job of the director's wife to make an annual trip to the local Christian bookstore to select a range of inspirational and instructional books, later to be packaged and sent surface mail to our many overseas workers as Christmas presents. "Remember," Bill was quick to point out, "since you've lived overseas, you're the one more likely to know which books will be most useful to our workers." And then, as if to clinch it with one more motivating tactic, he suggested, "Why not kill two birds with one stone and use this opportunity to look for suitable materials for your Bible study?"

But I simply wasn't interested in killing two birds with one stone, thank you very much! To my ever-capable, kill-at-least-two-dozen-dragons-with-one-stone husband, my reluctance to execute such a small "kill" as this was illogical, to say the least. Of course, what Bill didn't know and what I was loathe to admit even to myself was the exaggerated lack of confidence I felt for each of these tasks singly, let alone combined. As usual, instead of moving mountains through faith, I was manufacturing them out of molehills and accumulating mountains of pressure at the same time. And so to protect myself against my self-made overload, I remained stubbornly determined to deal with only one Goliath-sized task at a time.

The next morning, with *very* little enthusiasm and with even less dependence on God, I set out for the bookstore, all geared up to level Bill's assignment in one big whack, if at all possible, so that I could move on to the next weighty task—"such as *worry* over your Bible study?" chided a discerning inner voice that I chose to ignore.

As I wandered up and down the aisles of the shop, I felt decidedly swamped by what appeared to be a glut of books from which to choose. This swamped feeling was no longer agoraphobia itself, thank God, though it was perhaps one lingering emotional scar, reminding me of what once had been. Just then a clerk materialized in front of me and asked if she could be of any help. Only to oblige her, I explained my intentions, thinking all the while, *What can a complete outsider do but make things harder by loading me down with a lot of irrelevant suggestions?* After a while she annoyingly reappeared, clutching a number of books in her hand. As she proceeded to describe each one, I accommodated her yet again by muttering a few well-placed "I sees." It wasn't that I was ungrateful for her efforts, but I impatiently wanted to press on with my own heated search, prayerless and self-sufficient as it was.

As she held her last book in front of my inattentive eyes, I was scarcely prepared for the electrifying effect her words would have on me, for they literally jolted me to attention: "And just in case some of your overseas workers would like to get involved in neighborhood Bible studies . . ." she began. Next thing I knew, that book was out of her hands and into mine, nearly being turned inside out in my eagerness to know more. It was only a small paperback telling the story of its author, Winnie Christensen, and her exciting experience studying the Bible with her neighbors and seeing God do the incredible. The title of her book, curiously enough, was *Caught with My Mouth Open.*[1] "Sounds exactly like me at our first Bible study," I recalled with a heartening sense of identification. So Bill had had the right idea after all—clearly God's idea. In spite of myself, I indeed (though not I alone) was killing two birds with one stone! From one moment to the next I had shifted the burden of self-dependence back over to the Lord where it belonged. And from that moment of renewed God-dependence I virtually skateboarded around the bookstore, breathlessly following a string of further "leadings," which drew me from

---

[1] Wheaton, Ill.: Harold Shaw, 1969.

one choice book to another. In record time, I was driving home again, my car laden with a fascinating range of useful books for our overseas workers. Best of all, I was going home with some God-given guidance for our future Bible studies, but not without having had my knuckles rapped soundly by the Holy Spirit for slipping back into my pathetic self-sufficiency. And why had I done it? Not because I had thought *I* was so capable—certainly not that—but because I had doubted that *He* was capable. Or more precisely, I had doubted that He could or would exercise His capability in and through *me*. And so I had limited myself to the only resource I felt sure of: the resource of my own puny self. I was dying to share all this with Shirley, and with Bill just as much. In spite of my original negative outlook, I knew I was safe with him. Those tantalizing words, "I told you so," simply were not part of Bill's vocabulary; instead, he liked to use terms of joy and excitement, like "fantastic!"

And fantastic it was indeed. Before I had reached the halfway mark in Winnie's book, a tiny footnote naming the publisher of the study guide she had used jumped off the page and grabbed my attention: "Neighborhood Bible Studies, Inc., Dobbs Ferry, N.Y." At that point, only God knew the difference that footnote was to make, not only in the future of our Bible study, but also in my own future life of service. After chatting about it with Shirley, we decided to go for this material, believing we were being led by the Lord. This sent me straight back to our local Christian bookstore and back to that helpful clerk, this time not to oblige her, but to thank her, to laugh with her, and to praise the Lord with her.

For the second time that week, I drove home with a selection of books in the car: an ample supply of discussion guides based on the gospel of Mark, plus several copies of *How to Start a Neighborhood Bible Study,* which Shirley and I later pored over. This remarkable Neighborhood Bible

Studies (NBS) material, designed to be used as a tool for evangelism, had been pioneered and written by two ladies who, like Winnie Christensen, were completely unknown to us: Marilyn Kunz and Catherine Schell. Whoever they were, we already loved them for providing exactly what we, and perhaps countless others like us, needed in order to get involved in the outreaching purposes of God in our neighborhood.

Finally the day came to restart our Bible study. Gathering ourselves once more around our beloved oval table, Shirley and I began to read out important points from our now well-worn copies of *How to Start a Neighborhood Bible Study,* such as: "This group is *not* for experts—it's for those who don't know much about the Bible but who would like to discover for themselves what the Bible says." To the relief and encouragement of us all, these words described our group as if written for us alone.

Drawing again from our how-to book, we went on to explain further, "You know, ladies, the Bible is not just a collection of verses, as many people suppose; it's actually a collection of individual books, rather like a library. These books were meant to be read from start to finish, at least initially, just as one would read any other book, or even a letter. And this is how we'd like to approach the Bible in our group, not jumping around to different verses, but focusing on one book at a time. For our first book, as recommended by the NBS material, we're going to be studying the shortest, fastest-moving gospel, the gospel written by Mark."

Spurred on by a number of encouraging facial expressions around the table, Shirley and I proceeded to hand out the discussion guides on Mark. As the ladies began to leaf through them, we let them know that this was not going to be a lecture series, but rather a series of informal discussions, aided by questions from the study guides that they now held in their hands. This made an ideal moment to introduce a rather interesting, if somewhat unorthodox, feature of the NBS method: The *leader* of each Bible study is *not* the teacher, but merely the "question asker," who simply *reads out* the questions in the discussion guide and leaves it to the others to answer them. That is all!

"In other words, ladies," we quipped (but they knew we were serious), "the only qualification needed to be a leader is the ability to read!"

We went on to emphasize once more that the group members, not the leader, would answer the questions, but with one important ground rule in mind: "the answers to all questions are to be drawn from the Bible passage being examined, not from our own opinions or preconceived ideas."

In support of that ground rule, we all agreed to resist the temptation to quote from other authorities, such as the local clergy, the *Reader's Digest,* a favorite auntie, or some film or book. Whether or not we believed the Bible to be true, *we were to let the Bible speak for itself.*

By now the group was with us all the way, for this method, though new to our thinking, already held great appeal for each one of us. That appeal lay in the fact that by design, the method was user-friendly, even among the most uninitiated, and at the same time it guarded against the mishandling of Scripture.

I began to feel something stir inside me, a sense of exhilaration similar to the feeling one gets standing at the seashore. There seemed nothing left for us as a group to do but to wade in and start getting our spiritual feet wet. Our common bond was this: we were all learners (me included), all pieces of pliable putty, clay being bonded to clay in the Potter's hands. This motley fellowship of earthen vessels gave us the collective closeness we needed, not only with each other but also with the Lord, to step out as one into the bracing waters of discovery. And this we were just about to do, except for being held back momentarily by Bev—or was it really the Lord?

"Joanie and Shirley . . ." she broke in hesitantly, not wishing to intrude, yet obviously feeling compelled to do so, "do you think we could include something else when we meet? Do you think we could have that time of silent prayer for each other, like we had the first time? I really need that . . . maybe we all do." Others around the circle either nodded or murmured in agreement.

Why hadn't I dared to suggest this? Why was I so often cautious, such a mustn't-put-people-off sort of person? On the other hand, hadn't we been outspoken about our goal to make this everybody's Bible study rather than Shirley's and Joanie's? Yes, and Bev had taken us at our word. More than that, though Bev probably hadn't realized it at the time, her heartfelt plea for prayer underscored our much greater goal: that this should be the *Lord's* Bible study.

And so for the second time, a time as alive and real as the first, heaven bent down and blessed our patch of earth in response to our up-reaching, wordless prayers. Once the "Amen" had been spoken, we felt a bit more ready to take the plunge into our first proper Bible study. At the beautiful sound of those first questions being read out from our study guides and the even sweeter sound of those first, timid answers being echoed back, drawn thoughtfully from our Bibles, I knew that all this was explainable only in terms of God, the living God who *still today* is "able to do immeasurably more than all we ask or imagine, according to his power that is at work within us" (Eph. 3:20 NIV).

Next time we met, just before our period of silent prayer, one lady shared the difficulty she was having remembering all the items on our growing list of needs as she prayed. Others seemed to be having similar difficulty, yet all were determined not to slight anyone's shared need. At that point, I found myself volunteering to keep a written record of all the prayer needs mentioned so far and to read them out very slowly each week during our time of silent prayer. Even as I made this suggestion and saw it being accepted enthusiastically, I secretly began to question how long we should continue with our silent prayer experiment. True, God had proved that He didn't need our audible words, but still, might He not prefer them? On the other hand, we felt it wouldn't be right to turn our gathering into a traditional, often long-winded prayer meeting. Not only would this steal too much time away from our priority of Bible study, it would put undue pressure on our neighbors to pray aloud, or more likely still, create a situation where most people would sit back and let Shirley and me do all the praying.

Several weeks later I experienced another moment of unease as Bev presented a prayer request concerning her youngest son. This request was a "biggie," taking us well beyond the general, run-of-the-mill prayers for added wisdom, patience, or strength, many of which we believed had received tangible answers. "I really would appreciate your prayers that God would heal Danny's legs," Bev appealed boldly with her usual matter-of-fact faith. "He's got Blount's disease—that's 'bowed legs'—and the only treatment is to wear special shoes every night that are joined together with a steel brace. They're supposed to be child-proof, but Danny manages to strip them off night after night. It's a hopeless situation . . . unless God heals."

No one, but *no one* around the table so much as batted an eye at Bev's prayer request—unless it was Shirley or me. By now, of course, we were well into the gospel of Mark in our group studies, and we were loving it. Not only that, everyone was being careful, as agreed from the start, to let the Bible speak for itself. As far as our neighbors were concerned, letting the Bible speak for itself quite naturally included this matter of physical healing as much as anything else, for healing was part of Mark's gospel. It never crossed their minds to question whether or not Jesus healed people today, or whether our unspoken prayers with only an "Amen" tacked on at the end were a suitable channel for such healing. No, in their unspoiled minds, anything Jesus did then, we could beseech Him to do here and now, and through the simplest of faith. I didn't wish to argue with that, for I myself had always believed in God's power to heal. And yet, when I thought about it, believing that God *can* heal is somehow a long way from believing that He *will* heal or that He necessarily *wants* to do so.

"Thank you so much for sharing that, Bev," I responded in a noncommittal way as I jotted down the words, "healing for Danny's legs." Then looking around the table, I forged ahead in an unruffled manner with, "Any other new requests this morning?" Moments later, during our silent prayers, I was aware that while everyone else was asking the Lord to make Danny's legs better, I was worrying about what to do and what to say in God's defense in case He didn't.

In the meantime, week after week came and went, chapter after chapter was studied, prayer after silent prayer was prayed, and all the while our numbers were building. To accommodate this welcome growth, we eventually had to add a second row of "sanctified" chairs around our table. We soon noticed, however, that the increase in numbers reduced the level of participation we previously had enjoyed, along with its many benefits. After some thought and prayer, Shirley and I decided we should bring up the idea of dividing our group in half, letting Shirley take her people back to her neighborhood and leaving those from our neighborhood with me. This was in the hope that such division might have a multiplying effect, giving the two smaller groups a chance to experience their own growth and, if it came to that, the motivation to divide yet again. We knew full well, of course, that to the others such an idea would be just about as welcome as suggesting an amputation of an arm or a leg. What response, then, would we get to our suggestion? Outright resistance? Reluctant compliance? We looked forward to neither one.

Again we underestimated our astonishing neighbors. In one respect we had been right, for as we broached the subject, expressions of dismay clouded their faces and a barely audible "Oh no" slipped out from under someone's breath. But after a period of discussion between themselves, they were united in a moving rejection of the "holy huddle" mentality in favor of a spirit of self-giving. As they began to come around to this oneness of spirit, someone took the lead and began summarizing on behalf of everybody: "To be honest, Shirley and Joanie, I think all of us would rather keep things exactly as they are. We've grown really close to one another, plus we're learning so much through being part of this special group." Nods from all sides let her know that these were indeed their sentiments. "And yet . . ." she went on thoughtfully, with a tone of conviction in her voice, "there must be many others out there who need what we've got, and personally, I long to see them have it." With even more energetic nods of agreement giving her the go-ahead to wrap it up for everyone, she concluded: "If dividing is the way to give them that chance, then I say, let's do it."

And they were as good as their word. In the faith that their tough decision would increase rather than diminish the size of the group, they agreed to take this step without delay. In response to their faith, the Lord was also as good as His word, that word of His that promises, "According to your faith be it unto you" (Matt. 9:29). In no time at all and in both groups, He saw to it that any gaps created through dividing were closed up again by an increase of newcomers.

On and on went our weekly twin Bible studies, our guided discussions, our silent prayers, stretching out into months of successive spiritual landmarks: a number of stammering but sincere confessions of faith in Christ, stories of improved family relationships through personal inner change, signs of certain strains and stresses giving way to more restful trust in God and His Word.

In the meantime, our bold Bev was showing no signs of let-up in her faith as she kept urging us on in our prayers for Danny's legs. At the same time, without setting out to do so, I found myself doing some behind-the-scenes homework in the area of healing. This homework compelled me to reflect more openly on the Scriptures we were handling as a group and to face more squarely the wide range of human need represented in our group. As I did this, I began to pick up some important "subjective truths" that tend to be swallowed up, sadly, by some equally important "objective truths." For instance, contrary to some of the previous teaching I had received, I began observing in the Gospels that the purpose of Jesus' healing was not *always* or *only* to demonstrate the objective truth that He is the Son of God, central as this truth is. If that had been His sole purpose—to establish His identity and authority through healing—then the accounts of His many healings in the gospels have satisfied this purpose so that healing itself is no longer ever needed, only our belief in what He once did and why He did it. On the other hand, my observations showed me that sometimes, perhaps more often than not, Jesus *also* healed in demonstration of a more subjective truth—the tender truth of His compassion for the person in need. The question I felt Him putting to me was this: did I have like compassion for the afflicted, enough compassion to remove healing from the realm of theory and, like any other gift of God's grace, to pray for its release—or at least an *opportunity* for its release—in the realm of personal experience?

One weekend we visited Bill's home church in Wooster, Ohio, where we heard a beautiful sermon as part of a communion service. The pastor of the church pointed out in simple terms that it was Christ's death on Calvary that had paid for everything that God ever would wish to supply in the lives of His children. As that humble servant stepped down from the pulpit and stood before the communion table, he began to prepare the elements while speaking these words of invitation: "As God's beloved family gathered here, we represent a host of needs. Whatever your own needs are, God longs for you to accept His Son's death as full payment for those needs and their supply. As you take, eat, and drink of these symbols, remember that it was for *us* that He died . . . and by faith, *make full use of Calvary.*"

As I bowed my head, I felt totally enclosed in God's presence. Opening my Bible on my lap, I re-read familiar words from Isaiah 53, the chapter prophesying Christ's vicarious suffering on the cross: "Surely he took up our infirmities . . . and by his wounds we are healed" (vv. 4-5, NIV) Moving from the Old Testament to the New, I turned to similar words in Matthew 8:17. In fact, in this verse Matthew was quoting Isaiah in order to give prophetic support to the many healings that he had seen Christ perform, both spiritual and physical: "This was to fulfill what was spoken through the prophet Isaiah: 'He took up our infirmities and carried our diseases' " (NIV).

"Make full use of Calvary." This was God's latest message to me concerning dependence on Him, and that message was giving rise to another of those God-given, first-time-ever prayers in me, in fact it was one of those "dubious" silent prayers: *Lord, I've already received you as my Savior and Lord. I've also known you as my Teacher and Counselor. But today, Lord, I wish to acknowledge you as my Healer, whatever that may mean.* I had only just begun to find out what His healing could mean, mainly through my own inner healing, which was still going on. My continued pill-taking was one remaining area that I knew was awaiting His timing and touch. *I believe you have come to meet and heal your people at every level of need—body, soul, and*

spirit, I continued to pray within myself. *Some of that healing will come to us on earth, and some in heaven. But whether sooner or later, Lord, I believe ultimate wholeness is ours . . . and all because of Calvary. Please Lord . . . please don't let your sufferings on Calvary be in vain in my life . . . please teach me how to make full use of Calvary in all things . . . including this matter of pills.*

As we drove back to West Chicago, I still felt somewhat unsure, though no longer uneasy, about the healing of Danny's legs. A few weeks later, Bev breezed in to announce breathlessly that at Danny's last check-up, the doctor had noticed a slight straightening in those two bowed legs. Though he in no way saw this as a hopeful sign, Bev, on the other hand, was confident that this was the beginning of the healing for which we had been praying, and she plainly told him so.

In the weeks that followed, while we kept on examining the good news of Jesus according to Mark's gospel, we were being brought the good news of Jesus according to Bev—the good news of Danny's improving legs.

Then came that unforgettable morning when we gathered once more around our oval table and listened to Bev as she joyfully delivered a long-awaited message: "Danny's legs . . . they've been pronounced 'normal'! The consultant was baffled, of course, but he ended up agreeing with my explanation—the only explanation there is—that God has healed Danny through prayer!" In that moment, a number of ladies found themselves exercising spontaneous, audible prayer for the very first time as this one and that offered up a joyful, "Thank you, God!" or "Praise the Lord!" In the midst of our rejoicing, the message of Calvary was breaking through afresh to me: we are guilty of wasting the death of Christ, even disgracing it, unless we begin to make use of what His agonizing death has won for us.

Inexperienced Bev had made full use of Calvary, fuller use than I so far had made of it, and I knew God was speaking to me through her. He was telling me that I must never again set aside the possibility of physical healing as I'd formerly done. At the same time, I knew I wasn't being pulled from one narrow extreme to the other, from a view that God *never* heals to the view that He *always* heals. No, instead of narrowness in either direction, I was being *enlarged* and *opened* to all sides of God's grace—grace that has the power to bless afflicted people, here and now, with glorious physical healing, and grace that is no less glorious in its ability to transfigure a host of equally blessed people for whom (at least this side of heaven) physical healing doesn't come.

For our Danny, however, physical healing *had* come this side of heaven. And it was his healing, plus our incredible neighborhood experience, that God had used to stamp this widened view of dependence on God indelibly on my heart.

Kicking the Habit

7

"You're well now, you know."
These exact words, including the "you know" part, took me by complete surprise one morning as I was about to swallow one of my three-a-day tranquilizers. This was definitely some inside information, a "word from the Lord" spoken quietly from within me, yet in a tone so clear that it may as well have been shouted from the housetops.

I am? I answered back incredulously. Could it really be that this all-too-familiar, small, round, white object gripped between my thumb and forefinger was about to lose its grip on *me* at long last?

Instead of dropping the tablet down my throat, I decided to drop it back into the bottle, at least for the moment, while I sat down to do some thinking. Recalling my first guilt-ridden days of pill-taking, I reminded myself of the one acceptable rationale I had given myself for taking them, expressed in an earnest prayer I had prayed only once, but had never retracted nor forgotten: "Lord, I know these pills are not the answer; they deal only with my symptoms and not with the cause of my symptoms. *Please deal with the cause, Lord,* so that I'll be well and no longer need these wretched things!" And now, a full five years later, these words had come, *"You're well now, you know."* Was God saying that my prayer of so long ago was now an *answered* prayer? Had He dealt with the cause of my symptoms so thoroughly since then that, in His eyes, I was whole enough to throw away my tablets?

This seemed the obvious conclusion to make, especially in view of all the events that had taken place since that prayer had been prayed. The most recent and far-reaching event, of course, had been the formation of our neighborhood Bible study. As I thought about our remarkable neighbors, who for the last two years had gathered week by week around our table discussing the writings of Mark, Luke, and now theological Paul as naturally as they discussed child-rearing, diaper rash, or the price of eggs, I was taken back to my Geneva "snapshot." What I had glimpsed two and a half years earlier on the walls of my troubled mind—a group of faceless ladies sitting around a table studying the Bible—was now a live event that was taking place week after week before my very eyes. I knew, however, that this live event was not something that was happening only to others, while I played the role of spectator. Far from it. The Lord had shown me shortly before our first Bible study that this group was meant to be for my good as much as for the good of others. Now, much later, it was perfectly clear that a large portion of this "good" had come to me in the form of ever-increasing wholeness, just as the Lord had intended.

It was already during our first month of meeting together that the earliest evidence of increased wholeness began showing itself. It took no longer than that to recognize that my week in, week out involvement with my neighbors was forcing me to spend more time thinking about others and less time thinking about myself—*a lot* less time. At the end of my busier days, I was often pleasantly surprised to find that it had been hours since I had given more than a passing thought to myself and my own welfare, a rather new experience for me. And yet my heart had kept right on beating, my blood had kept right on circulating, and my lungs had kept right on breathing in and out! In time I began to enjoy what the old hymn-writer described as "a heart at leisure from itself," perhaps the true essence of inner wholeness.

Glancing back over our years in Geneva, I noticed by way of comparison something I hadn't noticed before: for me personally, those years had been lived within a tightly woven cocoon of extreme self-preoccupation. Constricting though that cocoon had been, it was at least the one safe place of retreat I knew of. Or so it had seemed, until I began attaching my cocooned life to the security of our fourth-floor apartment. I hadn't realized this was happening, of course, much less did I anticipate the consequence—a full-blown case of agoraphobia. But joy of joys, God's unfolding healing had been an effective one, gradually severing my inner cocoon from the surrounding cocoon of our flat.

Although I remained free of my agoraphobia from then on, soon after our arrival in the U.S. I became oddly aware that I still lived in a self-preoccupied, self-protected cocoon—one that walked and talked and even shopped like other folk, and indeed was somewhat less self-absorbed than before—*but a cocoon nonetheless.* And yet, in the midst of all this the Lord had been at work, forming wings on my sluggish soul and causing those wings to struggle fiercely against the limiting walls of that cocoon. Finally, the demands of our neighborhood Bible study gave me the extra push I needed to break my cocoon wide open and, though they hardly knew it, my neighbors themselves were instrumental in drawing this delicate Madame Butterfly out of her stifling, self-contained prison!

So here I was, enjoying life outside the cocoon, no longer a Grand Canyon of bitterness, no longer feeling insane in the supermarkets, and apparently no longer needing to rely on tablets to see me through. An emotion of sheer relief began to well up in me, the sort of relief one feels at the end of a long, arduous journey when one can look back to see that the journey, though often discouraging, has not been in vain. Groping for adequate words after my rather long pause for thought, I finally said, *This is an indescribable moment, Lord—the moment I've waited for, trusted you for, worked with you for. As of right now, with faith in your word, I shall stop taking my tablets. Thank you, thank you, Lord, for making this step possible!*

As I stood to my feet and began moving into the day, I felt rather exposed and unprotected without my tablets. Uncomfortable as this was, it didn't alarm me, nor was I in any doubt that I would be all right, for I was well now. The Lord Himself had said so, and that was enough.

But as hour followed hour, mounting physical and emotional symptoms began to unnerve my every move, my every thought. By the end of the day I felt agitated, trembly, even frantic, swinging back and forth like a pendulum between hot and cold sensations. From somewhere inside me a gut-level emotion demanded to know why a supposedly well person should be going through all this. At that point I sought no answer, only momentary relief. Forgive me, Lord . . . another tablet.

So far, right or wrong, I hadn't shared my new initiative and its disappointing outcome with anyone, not even with Bill, since he happened to be traveling at the time. Now, at the end of this traumatic day, I had nowhere else to go but to God. Though I hadn't meant to, I was coming to Him yet again as a *last resort.* But at least He was the *best* of all resorts, whether first or last. At that late and lonely hour it comforted me to remember that God, our Keeper, is ever-present and ever-available, never away on a journey, never napping, never out to lunch. This was the God who had challenged me to make full use of Calvary for all my infirmities, even for this one. Without further delay I bowed in His presence. Feeling the full weight of my failure, I sensed no rebuke from Him, oddly enough, over the tablet I had just taken, only a question: *why* had I stopped my tablets without first referring to Him?

Yes, why had I? Having depended on tablets for so long, wasn't it unreasonable of me to expect that I could or should give up that dependence, even as a well person, without maintaining my dependence on the Lord? Why hadn't I gone straight to Him to seek further understanding and personal guidance? Only a short time ago I had read a quotation that painfully applied to me: "A fool does in the end what a wise person does in the beginning." Today I had been that foolish one, for I had been presumptuous. I had accepted the Lord's pronouncement of wholeness, which was a right thing to do, but I had acted on it self-sufficiently, which was a wrong thing to do. *I'm so* very sorry, *Lord,* I prayed in deep contrition. *Please forgive me.* In the full assurance of my forgiveness, I went on to affirm, *I still believe your word to me, Lord, that I really am well. But I need* your *wisdom,* not mine, *to show me the way forward.*

As always, the very moment I began to depend on the Lord, that was the moment He began to help me. To my relief, His own appraisal of my situation, realistic and concrete, now dawned on me. What He had known all along, I now also knew: although I was a well person and no longer needed to be propped up by pills, at the same time I was addicted to those small, round bits of compressed chemicals. How much of it was physical addiction and how much was psychological didn't seem an issue, only that I was addicted.

Remembering another prayer of so long ago: "Heal me *in such a way* that I can bring the same sort of healing to others," I felt no inclination to plead for a spiritual "zap" that would sweep the addiction away miraculously, possible though it was and convenient though it would be. At the same time I believed God had a solution for me, an equally Spirit-inspired solution that would be available to anyone in my position and in the long run would be just as effective, if not more so, than the miraculous sort.

Ignorant as I was of these matters, I now at least recognized that coming off my tablets "cold turkey" was going to require an interruption of my main responsibilities, for how long I didn't know, including those that were of vital help to Bill in his already overloaded, overcommitted life and ministry. This is what concerned me most of all. The sudden withdrawal of my tablets with its adverse symptoms was a process I was willing to go through as long as I had Bill's support, and I knew that he would move heaven and earth to give it. But I also knew how stressful this would be to him on top of everything else, a burden that I couldn't bear to lay on him, especially just now.

No sooner had I expressed this concern to the Lord than a plan began to formulate itself quickly in my mind, showing me another way to come off my tablets, along with the logic behind it. Reasoning aloud in prayer, I said thoughtfully, "Lord, I believe you're giving me an idea. What if I were to come off my tablets *very, very slowly*—so slowly that my mind and body didn't know it was happening. Then, surely, I wouldn't get those horrible physical and psychological reactions."

With that, I went into the kitchen and spread all my tablets on the bread board. Searching in a drawer for our sharpest knife, I thought in good humor, *Now I know why these tablets have a crease down the middle!* One after the other I began cutting them carefully in half, then into quarters. And back into the bottle they went.

I crawled into bed that night almost eager for my restart tomorrow, not presumptuously as before, but this time in collaboration with the Lord. Here was the plan as I had thought it through and talked it through in His presence: Since my morning tablet was the one I seemed to need the least, that was the one from which I would cut away that first "unnoticeable quarter." After a few days (or whatever seemed comfortable), I would take a quarter away from my midday tablet as well, and later on again, from my evening tablet, so that eventually I would be taking three-quarters of a tablet three times a day. This I began to do, making no big deal out of it, but simply "doing the plan" and refusing to give it any undue attention. After all, my mind and body mustn't find out what I was up to! This left me free to go on living with "a heart at leisure from itself" and at the same time knowing the job was getting done, slowly but surely.

It wasn't long until, using the same method of reduction (one-quarter at a time), my tablets had been whittled down to half. And still I was steady! One day I remarked to Bill in passing, "I've got a surprise for you; I've been coming off my tablets."

For a moment Bill looked seriously into my eyes and then with loving concern he cautioned, "Be careful, honey. Don't make yourself ill, will you?"

"That's the wonderful thing about it, Bill," I responded happily. "Not only has the Lord shown me that I don't need these tablets anymore, He's also shown me how to come off them without getting ill."

After sharing with him the whole story and "the plan," which was still in operation but was so full of promise, I heard from Bill's lips the one word I was longing to hear: "Fantastic!" Then he bent over my five-foot-two frame and swallowed me up in a huge, six-foot-three hug that communicated something nonverbal to me. That something was our oneness as a couple, but it was far more than a physical oneness. It was *the union of years* that I was feeling, a union that comes only after years of shared struggle, and it was now being sealed by our shared faith for the approaching victory.

And victory did come. Needless to say, it was one of those little-by-little victories, which, since then, I've come to realize is sometimes God's preferred way with His people. Certainly it was His method with the children of Israel as they faced a host of enemies on their way to the Promised Land. Concerning these enemies, God had said; "Little by little I will drive them out before you, until you have increased enough to take possession of the land" (Exod. 23:30 NIV).

Likewise, this enemy of mine was being driven out of my system little by little, until eventually I was all the way down to one-quarter of a tablet to be taken three times a day. I very nearly decided to do away with this final stage and call it good. But no, I decided to fulfill the plan right down to the last, solitary quarter, for not one corner of victory was to be assumed. It was to be *won* by depending on God no less faithfully than I had depended on those wretched tablets.

Finally the last foothold of this enemy was overcome, and there was no more plan to fulfill. For several weeks I still carried a bottle of spare tablets in my handbag, feeling a bit safer just knowing they were there, yet at the same time knowing I wouldn't touch them. Then one day on my way out of the house, I pulled the bottle from my bag and shoved it into my kitchen cupboard next to my spices and herbs. And there it stayed, not just that day but for many days to come.

Weeks later, without particular forethought, I stopped one day at that same kitchen cupboard and brought the bottle down. I knew full well what I was about to do, and I was ready to do it. Removing the lid, I marched the bottle straight to the bathroom and, without further ado, flushed away the remaining tablets into the belly of the earth where they belonged.

That day I crossed over into my own drug-free land of promise and never looked back. It was no doubt a land with a few more giants to conquer, but conquer them I would, just as I had conquered this one—in dependence on God. But oh, how I longed to depend on Him more consistently. Apparently this was God's longing as well, for it soon proved to be the next item on His agenda.

Who's in Charge Here?

8 I was fond of our house in West Chicago for a number of reasons, not least of all for its remarkable kitchen floor. What I particularly liked about it was its rather nondescript grayish color, which meant that it was hard to tell if it was dirty, or for that matter, if it was clean. And so, according to convenience, "a lick and a promise" was sometimes all it got. Eventually, of course, the day of reckoning would come. A closer look or a prick of conscience would inform me that a few licks of a damp mop were no longer enough, that it was time I got down on my hands and knees and gave it the bucket and brush treatment.

So there I was one day, clad in a pair of old jeans and systematically scrubbing my way backwards across the kitchen floor on my knees. Suddenly, out of the blue, came a distinct impression that I should visit one of my neighbors named Carol, a young mom and a regular attender of our weekly Bible study. I don't think I initially took this impression as anything more than a feeling, so I carried on scrubbing and casually thought, *Perhaps it would be a good idea to drop in on Carol later today.*

But the impression returned, this time more strongly than before, alerting me to treat it as a prompting from the Lord and pressing me to *definitely* visit Carol that afternoon. *But first I must finish this floor,* I thought to myself with unwavering dedication to the task at hand.

As I continued to scrub, the impression began to take on a tone of urgency, which made it less like a prompting and more like "orders from headquarters." *As soon as I finish scrubbing the floor,* I assured the Lord, *I'll change my clothes and go right down to Carol's.* But deep inside, something (or Someone) told me that later wasn't what the Lord had in mind. He meant *now, before* the floor was finished!

During the next few moments, as I rested on my suds-soaked knees, a real battle of wills took place. In some ways, this call to visit Carol wasn't particularly new. I often thought of things I longed to do or felt led to do for others. But invariably there was something else I needed to do first, usually something less important but somehow more pressing. This dilemma of lost opportunities disturbed me so much that some time earlier I had made a blanket resolution: once I'd gotten the house properly cleaned and my ironing caught up and my backlog of letters written, *then* I would start responding to these inner impulses. To my chagrin, I had to admit that, so far, my unrealistic ideal hadn't been realized and probably never would be.

Clearly, this impulse to visit Carol and to do it now was one of those moments when something less important seemed more pressing—namely, finishing my kitchen floor. But was that so unreasonable, I asked myself? After all, what if Bill or the girls or, worse yet, unexpected visitors were to come to find a sudsy, half-scrubbed kitchen floor? What would they think of me and my sloppy housekeeping? In any case, surely the quarter of an hour or so it would take to finish the job wouldn't make that much difference.

There was no doubt about it, quite apart from visiting Carol and the question of when, I was being confronted with another all-important question: "Who's in charge here? God or me?" This was a test and I knew it, a challenge to say no to my insecure need for ideal circumstances, to say no to my independent mind-set, *to deny myself* as Jesus had taught, and to apply His teaching in the everyday, practical realm.

All right, Lord, I said as I stood to my feet in surrender, *I'll obey you; I'll go to Carol's* now. The choice to oppose the natural grain of my independence was an uncomfortable yet exhilarating step. The very act of turning my back on my half-scrubbed floor and heading down to Carol's house felt like a spiritual breakthrough. When I arrived and looked into her eyes, brimming with tears, and heard her say, "Joanie, how could you have known I needed you right this moment?" I knew it was a spiritual breakthrough for both of us. For Carol, as a disheartened and drained young mother, finding a friend at her doorstep the precise instant she needed to know that someone cared, made her realize that *God* cared. That day proved to be the beginning of Carol's surrender to Christ as Savior, and behind her surrender was a secret surrender of my own, a willingness to let God be God, to let God be in charge—for the time being, at least.

For the time being. Ah yes, what *was* it about this underlying spiritual independence in me, that it kept jumping up time after time like an unruly dog and forever getting in the way of God being God in my life? With great effort I could get this "dog" to back down and even lie down, just as it had the day I visited Carol. But no way could I get it to stay down. In all truth, I was getting pretty disillusioned about this side of myself. In fact, I was beginning to wonder if my chronic pattern of independence was another one of those habits that, like my old bitterness habit and likewise my pill habit, needed to be kicked.

I knew from personal experience, of course, that the latter two habits could be broken. But what about this ingrained streak of spiritual independence? As far as I could tell, it seemed to be ingrained in every one of us to some degree, and I had to ask the question, Is it even *possible* for this God-resistant side of human nature, this "untamed, spoiled dog" within us, to be put in its place this side of heaven? Suddenly I remembered yet another prayer I had prayed during Geneva days, but this one I had totally forgotten until now. As a background to that prayer, I remembered wading through chapters 6, 7, and 8 of Romans, a trilogy of chapters that deal with some pretty tricky subjects—our "old" and "new" natures, our need to be dead to sin and alive to Christ, the dilemma of wanting to do good and yet often doing what is wrong, and the call to live in the Spirit rather than in the flesh. Sensing that these three chapters held a vital key for Christian living, I had made up my mind to dissect and analyze them, almost like a scientist, determined not to give up until I came up with that key.

With amusement I remembered the single-minded way I had taken pen and paper in hand and made an impressive use of squiggly lines, circles, squares, triangles, and even little stick men, all in a feverish attempt to diagram and apply the material in these three chapters. But every time I thought I'd gotten it, I realized I hadn't. Then I recalled giving up my futile efforts and praying this prayer instead, a prayer I weighed carefully before offering it up: "Lord, if these chapters are as important as I believe they are, then *whatever it takes*" (that was the part I weighed) "and *however long*, please help me to understand them." Then I left the prayer with Him, really left it, forgetting that I had prayed in this way. But God hadn't forgotten. And now, a few years later, years that contained a perfect mix of "all that it had taken" in time and testing, He was directing me back to these chapters.

As I reopened my Bible to Romans 6, 7, and 8 and began reading, the understanding that had eluded me years before began to rise slowly like oil on water. Grabbing pen and paper again, I wondered why this time it was different, why this time spiritual insights were practically dripping off those once dry, unyielding pages. Certainly my well-established commitment to read, pray, trust, and obey as a daily discipline had heightened my capacity to grasp spiritual truth. And certainly that spiritual capacity had become more teachable every time I experienced a breakthrough in my dependence on God, inconsistent though my practice of it still often was.

Before reading any further, I found myself singling out one familiar verse, Romans 8:16, as if laying a cornerstone on which to build. This particular verse was special to me, for it was the very first one that "lit up" for me after becoming a Christian at age seventeen: "The Spirit himself testifies with our spirit that we are God's children" (NIV).

When I came across those words as a brand new Christian, I thought excitedly, *That's what I experienced the night I received the Lord—God witnessing to my heart that I now belonged to Him,* which is surely what the common phrase "assurance of salvation" is all about.

Now that same verse was lighting up for me again, but this time I was being shown something I never had noticed before, the mention of two spirits—*God's Spirit* acting upon *our spirit.* Until that moment, the fact of God's Spirit within us was the only truth I had considered. Now, for the first time ever, I was seeing a corresponding truth: we have within us a human spirit of our own that God put there—a spiritual capacity, if you like, that was created by Him to be His dwelling place, His vehicle of communication and His impulse center *inside us.*

And something else clicked into focus as well. I now understood that this human spirit of ours is the essential and eternal us, though its universal condition is described by the apostle Paul as spiritually dead, or at least dead to God (Eph. 2:1; 4:17-18). It is dead and in darkness, Paul informs us, because of sin, our own personal sin. Since God and sin cannot dwell together, a chasm has come between our spirit and its one and only source of life—God's Spirit.

Obviously, our only hope is to find our way back to our Source through repentance and conversion to Christ. That much I knew. I also knew that in order to be converted there is a part we must play, for conversion means to turn around, and *we* must do the turning. But little had I understood, except in vague terms, what God's part in conversion is. Now, however, something was beginning to dawn on me—that as we turn *from* sin and *to* God, the same power that raised Jesus up from the dead raises our deadened spirit back to life again and sets it free. At this thought, a cluster of lines from one of my favorite Charles Wesley hymns, "And Can It Be," surfaced in my mind:

> Long my imprisoned spirit lay
> Fast bound in sin and nature's night;
> Thine eyes diffused a quickening ray,
> I woke, the dungeon flamed with light;
> My chains fell off, my heart was free;
> I rose, went forth, and followed Thee.

I felt my heart skip a beat. *These words back up my very thoughts; they describe conversion as an inner resurrection, a resurrection of our spirit through God's Spirit!*

As if this realization were not mind-boggling enough, I found myself grasping something more: not only is our inner spirit raised up to life eternal, it is raised up *in the likeness of Christ*. Peter the apostle had made this same point in one of his letters (2 Peter 1:4), telling us that God's "great and precious promises" have been given to us so that we might be "partakers of the divine nature." Clearly all of this makes up that inner awakening described by Jesus as "being born again" or *"Spirit giving birth to spirit."*

This new chunk of information (new to me, that is) concerning our spiritual anatomy struck a responsive chord in me. I felt like singing and shouting Mary's opening line in the Magnificat: "My soul glorifies the Lord and my spirit rejoices in God my Savior"! (Luke 1:46-47, NIV). So this is what Jesus had in mind when He spoke to the woman at the well about worshiping God "in spirit and in truth." Along with this new insight came a new conviction:

> I am meant to be living the whole of my life in and through this awakened, reborn spirit of mine, and the key to such a life simply has to be wrapped up in *my* spirit learning to depend more wholly on *God's* Spirit—a true cooperation of spirit with Spirit.

I seemed to be on the right track at last, thanks to God's power of revelation at work in me. Now, instead of willfully wading through these chapters as I had done formerly, I sensed the Holy Spirit giving me a guided tour through them, that I might see things as He saw them. As so often in the past, He again was making me His student, seeking to get my thinking straight as a basis for getting my living straight. And I, His willing student, was being counted ready at last to begin grasping a few prickly nettles in Romans 6, 7, and 8.

For some light relief from all the concentration and spiritual excitement, I went into the kitchen and poured an extra large mug of coffee. *Looks like this is going to be some coffee break!* I mused as I headed back to my open Bible and unfinished notes. Resettling myself comfortably in the waiting presence of my Tutor, I turned back to Romans, chapter 6. As expected, I found my first nettle in verse 6: Paul's phrase, "our old self" (NIV), together with his statement that our old self had been crucified with Christ.

Exactly as before, the whole idea of being crucified *with Christ* still seemed like one of those difficult-to-understand and therefore difficult-to-apply mysteries. But now, however, accepting the mystery seemed more needful than understanding it—simply accepting that when Christ was crucified on the cross for our sins, God somehow "computed" the death of our old sinful self *into the death of*

His Son. By this God apparently was saying that He did not intend to do business with our old self but wished to write it off in its entirety on the cross.

At first this seemed a bit harsh of God. On the other hand, I had to admit that it seemed the surest way, no doubt the only way for God's magnificent alternative to emerge—the raising up of a totally "new self" in us. (Paul uses this term in Eph. 4:24 and in Col. 3:10.) Just as our old self had been computed into Christ's death, likewise this new self had been computed into Christ's resurrection, a new self that is raised up the moment a person is born of the Spirit. The *seat* of that new self—of this I was now sure—is our newborn spirit within us. And the *nature* of that new self is none other than the nature of Christ, fully endowed, of course, with all the qualities and abilities of Christ (wisdom, knowledge, power, and love, to name only a few), and all of these at our disposal.

From Romans 6, I was led on to chapter 7, where Paul again speaks of our old self but gives it a different name: the "sinful nature" (NIV), or in some translations, "the flesh." At this point the plot suddenly thickens in Paul's writing. Here, in shameless and self-revealing honesty, the apostle becomes vulnerable by writing about *his* old nature.

I was touched with empathy as I read of his own recurring dilemma, a dilemma exactly like mine, that of intending to do good but often doing wrong instead. He acknowledges within his body "another law," a law of sinful desires that dwells alongside the law of the Spirit. How comforted I felt to read that Paul himself, the powerful apostle, had known what it was to have this law gaining the upper hand in him, even to the point of making Paul a prisoner of his old, carnal self, which in turn had waged war against his higher, spiritual self (Rom. 7:23).

With an encouraging sense of identification I went on to read Paul's gutsy, global cry, the cry of all such exasperated believers: "What a wretched man I am! Who will rescue me from this body of death?" (NIV). And then in the next breath, he gives us his answer, equally global in scope: "Thanks be to God—through Jesus Christ our Lord!" (NIV).

Paul's universal question and answer landed me in chapter 8, which turned out to be the next crucial step toward tackling my "spoiled dog dilemma." In verses 5 and 7 he bluntly states that our sinful nature, with its sinful mind, is hostile to God. "It *does not* submit to God's law," he writes, *"nor can it do so"* (NIV, emphasis mine).

At last I saw the origin of that untrained, spoiled dog within me that refuses to knuckle under. According to Paul, stubborn independence happens to be the chief trait of our old nature, an untrainable nature at that.

So it was positively acceptable to be disillusioned with this side of myself! Paul seemed to be saying, in so many words, "Go ahead and be disillusioned. I myself was the same." (Hadn't he just conceded in chapter 7 that there was not one iota of good in his sinful nature?) "Only make sure," he seems to warn, "that you get disillusioned enough to give up on yourself." Then, familiar as Paul was with our human aversion to giving up on ourselves, he reasons further in verse 12, ". . . we have an obligation—but it is not to the sinful nature, to live according to it" (NIV).

How had I missed the point of this verse for so many years? Why hadn't I noticed that I had been living much of my life as if I *owed* it to my old nature to obey its promptings, as if I *owed* it to my old self to let it be "top dog"? I almost laughed at the sheer audacity of such an idea.

In the meantime, it had become my unconscious habit to do exactly that, to obligate myself to my old nature with only spasmodic relief from its hold over me—like the day I visited Carol. And of course, unless a better alternative was available, there was no hope of ever really breaking its hold. But a better alternative was what these chapters were all about. The Spirit's guided tour had convinced me of that. And since there was an alternative to be had, then I was going to have it!

As I combed these chapters once more under the guidance of the Holy Spirit, three words, rather like spiritual keys, were being etched on my mind: *recognize, reckon,* and *respond.* Later, for easy recall, I found it helpful to think of them as the three Rs. Springing out of Paul's teaching and personal experience, these spiritual keys had been cut with well-defined edges so that we, like him, might not fail to unlock the door to God's alternative. To that end, here are the keys as I initially understood them and planned to use them:

First, I was to *recognize,* now and for the rest of my earthly life, that as a Christian there are two capacities in me vying for supremacy—my old self with its corrupt, sinful nature and my new self with its boundless, Christ-like nature.

Second, in agreement with God's revealed perspective, I was to *reckon* my old self as crucified, dead, and buried with Christ and was to pronounce it dead in relation to sin. At the same time I was to *reckon* my new, regenerate self as raised up with Him and to count it alive in relation to righteousness. Such reckoning was to be an exercise of faith.

And third, I was to allow the Holy Spirit to translate my reckoning into personal experience as I exercised a *new, reversed response* toward these two vying selves in me. This reversed response (choosing to cater to my new self rather than my old) would render my old nature *unresponsive to sin,* day by day and choice by choice. As a result, my body would cease to be the unwitting instrument of my old nature as it so often had been; it would become the instrument of my new, Christlike nature instead.

In other words, since God viewed my old self as dead and since I was in total agreement with His view, day by day

I was to bring that death into effect by affording my old self no more rights and decision-making privileges than I would a corpse. Now, instead of obeying the promptings of my old self with its fleshly impulses, I was to treat it as dead and dare to say no to its clamorings. And as a dynamic alternative, I was to begin reaching out for the promptings of the Holy Spirit within my new self and boldly say yes to them. Since the whole idea of reckoning (along with recognizing and responding), was clearly God's idea, certainly not mine and not even Paul's, this wasn't merely the latest human-inspired how-to-get-it-right formula. Such formulas, I had noticed, tend to prey on people's spiritual discontent but seldom deliver the goods. No, this was a matter of believing and obeying God on God's terms as revealed in His Word and trusting the Holy Spirit to "make the reckoning good" within personal experience.

Great as my confidence was in the validity of these three keys, as yet they were totally untried by me. Faced with the challenge to put them to the test, I decided to take it on as an experiment, a "heavenly" experiment as I later called it. Since experiments usually are given a limited time-frame, I decided to allow myself one month for proving the difference this new effort could make in my Christian life. I also made a vow to conduct the experiment wholeheartedly and not to cheat or compromise along the way. At this point I bowed in God's presence and seriously prayed this prayer of commitment:

> Lord, up till now, Satan, self, and sin have prompted the old nature in me and instinctively I have obeyed. From now on it is my desire to say no to those promptings, and for this I claim your power. Please give me a recognition of the Holy Spirit's promptings in my new nature, that I may obey only Him. If at any time I fail in this, then by your Spirit help me to

recognize my failure so that I may confess it, receive your forgiveness, and immediately resume my living in the new nature.

As I threw myself into my experiment, I was grateful for the clear mechanics of what was mine to do. I couldn't help comparing it with my fairly recent experience of learning to drive a car. I remembered how foreign, indeed how forced every hand and foot movement had seemed during my early days of learning. But I also remembered how confident I'd been that with every concentrated effort, if practiced according to the book, driving would become more and more instinctive—perhaps even *second nature!*

As I proceeded to implement my experiment, I soon found out how disgustingly robust my old nature was and how pathetically feeble my new was. However, one stroll around our garden gave me the parable I needed to believe that this condition could be reversed. As I looked across our lawn and flower beds, I asked myself a preposterous question: *What would I need to do if I wanted a garden full of weeds? The answer was obvious: Nothing, nothing at all. All I would need to do is let things take their natural course, and an overgrown garden of robust weeds is what I would get.* For years that was how I had kept (or had *not* kept) the garden of my spiritual life. I had allowed things to take their natural course and had ended up with a weed-infested, dominant old nature on my hands. Again I looked at my garden and asked myself, *What would I need to do if I wanted a well-kept garden, free of weeds and full of healthy, productive plant life? Again the answer was obvious: I would need to take decisive action against all undesirable growth and actively cultivate that which is desirable.*

For the first time ever in my spiritual life, this is what God through His Word was equipping me to do. He was giving me the motivation and His very own method for starving my old nature of its life-sapping effects and for cultivating the life-giving power of the new. Or as this little rhyme so concisely puts it:

> Two forces surge within my breast—
> The one is foul, the other is blest;
> The "new" I love, the "old" I hate;
> The one I *feed* will dominate.

Days began to pass, revolutionary days they were, so that well before the allotted time of one month was up, I knew my experiment was ceasing to be an experiment and was becoming a way of life. In one sense this new way of life was not particularly exceptional, or at least it shouldn't have been. I had discovered things as they are meant to be, that's all, and was learning to function accordingly. Already my new nature was becoming stronger, for this was the one I was choosing to feed—time after time.

One particular example stands out in my memory. For a long time, for years in fact, I had been plagued by recurring doubts that I would ever be a whole person. On low days, one doubt after another would rise up within me and lodge itself stubbornly in my mind: *I'm not really getting better . . . I've been this way too long . . . I'm only kidding myself.* I longed to answer these doubts and somehow come against them, yet I simply hadn't known how. But now I did. Now I had a scriptural method—the three Rs—and I began putting them to work against these doubts.

First of all, I was able to *recognize* at last where those doubts came from. They came from me, of course, but from a particular side of me—from that old, self-centered, self-pitying nature within me. It was obvious that they didn't come from God, for these doubts were in total disagreement with His Word in this matter of inner wholeness. And His Word, not mine, was to be my frame of reference from now on.

Therefore, I had no obligation whatsoever to put up with these doubts. Instead I could (and did) *reckon* my doubting old nature as being crucified, dead, and buried with Christ, and I began treating it as such. In this case I chose simply to ignore it! At the same time I *reckoned* my new nature as being alive with Christ and therefore naturally inclined to listen to God's Word and agree with it.

And what was God's Word telling me? In Romans 8:6, I came upon a choice phrase: ". . . the mind controlled by the Spirit is life and peace" (NIV). "*Life and peace.*" These two words certainly described the inner wholeness I needed and longed for. And the words: *"the mind controlled by the Spirit"* were showing me the means for gaining and maintaining such inner wholeness.

The free *response* of my new nature that day was a resounding "Yes" and "Amen" to God's Word. From then on, I no longer allowed my old self to dominate my thoughts in this matter. As often as necessary I brought my mind under the Spirit's control through fresh applications of the three Rs. On the grounds of God's Word, not my fluctuating feelings, and within my new nature, not my old, I became more and more confident that it was only a matter of time until inner wholeness was mine, a confidence that would not be disappointed.

On and on I went in my experiment, bringing other areas of my mind under the control of the Holy Spirit. Whenever I caught myself operating in my old nature— feeling sorry for myself, magnifying problems through fear, holding back when I knew that I should be stepping out in faith—it was up to me to repent then and there and immediately take sides with God against that "spoiled dog" within me. As soon as that willful dog had been put in its place (something I found I could do anytime and anywhere as long as I was willing), I would turn my spirit toward the Holy Spirit within me (again something I could do anytime, anywhere). Drawing instantly close to Him and He to me, I would ask Him to prompt me within my new nature so that I might conform to His will in the situation.

Sometimes His promptings were fairly obvious to discern and obey, like exchanging my impatience for *His* patience, my unlove for *His* love, my inaction for *His* action. Others were more subtle, representing what we often call gray areas, when the right attitude or response in a given situation seems totally unclear. "But surely God Himself is never unclear about anything," I assured myself frequently. And since the Holy Spirit now had greater access to my spirit, there was nothing to hinder Him making all necessary promptings real to me, for now He could trust me with them.

It was during one of my moments of meditation that I first sensed His Spirit impress this rather new idea upon my spirit: *If I can* trust *you, I will* entrust *you,*" was the thought. All my life (and quite rightly, too), the necessity of *me* trusting *God* had been drummed into my thinking, along with a belief in His absolute trustworthiness. But here was something different—God *wanting,* strangely *needing* to trust *me!*

Outrageous as it seemed, I somehow knew what He was getting at. Once upon a time I hadn't a clue about Romans 6, 7, and 8 and those three spiritual keys. But now I did. Knowing something like that brings responsibility with it, and in God's eyes, fulfilling that responsibility was equivalent to personal trustworthiness. In other words, if He could trust me to live in accordance with what I now knew, then He would *entrust* me—*what with, I didn't yet know.* But one thing I did know, from now on nothing would be the same. I felt I was being given a before-and-after view of my life: *before* opening the door on God's alternative and *after, before* finding the keys to that door and *after, before* living in my new nature and *after.*

At the heart of it all, this basic issue of "who's in charge?" had been settled, at least potentially. No doubt it would have to be resettled more than once in the vast, uncharted territory that lay before me, for this was hardly a once-and-for-all matter. Yes, I *could* fail, certainly not a necessity, but a sad possibility nonetheless. Yet even in the event of failure, I at least would know what I had departed from, just as an experienced but careless driver may fail at driving. Yet like that irresponsible driver, I not only would know what I had departed from, I also would know what I must come back to—*back to the Book,* God's guide for our spiritual journey, and *back to its Author,* the God of all grace, forgiveness, and restoration.

Never again would I be able to plead ignorance. Sinfulness, yes, but never ignorance. Instead of ignorance I now had informed responsibilities to discharge, plus the promise of something up ahead, perhaps something to achieve *with God* and *for God.*

In the meantime, this repeated act of abandoning my old self to the grave and yielding my new self to the animating, controlling presence of the living Christ within me was becoming a dynamic pattern—a pattern of living more instinctively in my new nature and, at long last, living more consistently in dependence on God.

God's Alternative at Work

9 Now that I was depending on God more consistently, I found Him "talking to me" more easily—not that it's ever difficult for God to talk to His children and not that He hadn't talked to me before, for He had. It's just that until my discovery of God's alternative (learning to live in my new nature through "reckoning"), He had had to cut through my resistant old nature to reach the spiritual me and to overcome a real lack of cooperation due to my ignorance. Nowadays, however, His communications no longer came in spite of me, but much more *because of me,* for my renewed spiritual self was growing in the knowledge of God and was enjoying a two-way relationship with Him.

Like many of us, I was puzzled most of all by the communication side of this relationship. How did it work? How did God manage to speak to me without the use of audible words, and how did I manage to hear Him without the use of my two outer ears?

Quite unexpectedly I was helped in my understanding one day after I had laid some bread crumbs on my bird feeder and had stood at a nearby window to watch. Before long, one lone bird flew to the feeder, helped himself to a few choice crumbs, and then flew away. He must have done an effective job spreading the good news, for moments later a whole flock of birds descended on my feeder and made fast work of the remaining crumbs.

Exactly *how* had this little bird communicated his message to other birds, I wondered. Then this thought came to me: there's an entire bird kingdom out there, and in that kingdom it takes a bird to communicate with other birds. I still didn't know *how* that bird had communicated with the others, but I felt satisfied knowing *why* he had been able to do so. He had "talked to them" and they had understood his meaning because of their *alikeness.* He was a bird among birds.

The effect of that observation was to make me feel quite satisfied not to know exactly how God speaks to His children. It was enough to know that He was able to do so and why. God can "talk to us," His children, and we can understand His meaning because of our spiritual alikeness. Out of that alikeness God's Spirit and our spirit are able to interact with each other. Similar to those birds in our back yard, I saw that we Christians also live in a realm, a realm that is humming with spiritual communication. That realm is the kingdom of God. Surely this "law of alikeness" is what Paul was getting at in 1 Corinthians 2:11-12:

> For who among men knows the thoughts of a man except the man's spirit within him? In the same way no one knows the thoughts of God except the Spirit of God. We have not received [into our spirit] the spirit of the world but the Spirit who is from God, that we may understand [with our spirit's mind] what God has freely given us (NIV).

This, then, was the spiritual theory for interaction between God and me, but the keys that regularly turned that theory into experience were the three Rs, recognizing, reckoning, and responding. This was God's magnificent alternative *at work,* and I soon became impressed with its down-to-earth workability in real life.

For most of us, "real life" tends to be a life full of predicaments. (My own definition of a predicament is "predictable circumstances *gone wrong.")* In the face of this regular reality, God impressed some words on my spirit one morning as I sat reading my Bible and meditating: *"From now on, everything is part of progress in your life."* (By everything, I knew He meant those inevitable predicaments of life.)

Generally, God brought guidance to me mainly through the Scriptures, and very dynamically at times. But occasionally my Great Counselor would drop these one-liners in my direction to provoke my thinking in some needful way. This time He was putting His finger on my negative attitudes and provoking me to take a much more positive view of life's predicaments.

And provoking it was indeed, for I was a well-practiced moaner, groaner, and complainer. As a Christian, of course, I was careful to complain only when it seemed well-justified. Sometimes my complaints never escaped my lips, so that no one but God heard those mental moanings that usually went something like this: *Isn't it always the same—just when everything seems so perfect, then something has to come along and spoil it!* Or, *I can't believe this is happening to me—right in the middle of doing something so important, and I wasn't even doing it for myself!* To put it mildly, I detested this contrary side of life with its uncanny timing for messing things up at the worst possible moment. Up till now, I had felt I had every right to react as I did. After all, who needs all this frustration? *I* certainly didn't.

And yet, here was God telling me that I had no right at all to such a reaction. He wasn't exactly saying that I *needed* frustration, certainly not just for the sake of it. But what I *did* need was to be changed and to grow. His message, therefore, was this: life's predicaments are effective tools in His hand to bring about those changes in me. That was the sort of progress God's Spirit wanted for me. And once I got the message, this was what my spirit wanted as well. It was when my whimpering lower nature was in control that I loved to complain and feel sorry for myself. But in my higher, Christlike nature, I only wanted what God wanted. I wanted the same sort of progress described by Paul in Romans 5:3-4: ". . . we also rejoice in our sufferings, because we know that suffering produces perseverance; perseverance, character; and character, hope" (NIV).

At the same time, He showed me another important reason for dealing with my negative attitude: complaining over life's predicaments not only restricted His use of them in changing me, it also kept Him from doing something about the very predicaments I complained about. God was wanting to be actively at work within my own world of predicaments, and He was reminding me that He doesn't need ideal circumstances to achieve great things. Christ's agonizing death on the cross and all that He accomplished there was the ultimate proof of that.

However, before moving me out into the practicalities of this mental turnaround, God's Spirit dropped another one-liner into my spirit, and it was this: *"Don't let life happen to you; let life happen through you."*

How well the Lord knew me, for in the first part of this message, He was describing me to a T. I hadn't recognized it until now, but that was exactly how I saw life, as something that was coming at me from all directions. Feeling under threat much of the time, I had developed a defensive approach to life. Like a half-defeated warrior whose only tactic is to lift his shield against the onslaught of enemy arrows, I too was using all my energies to shield myself against the onslaught of life's hardships. Over the years, the language of such a life had become the language of complaint and self-pity.

But in the second part of His message, God was offering me an entirely different approach to life—to let life happen *through* me. Instead of fighting off all those fiery darts that seemed to be happening *to* me, I could let God's own river of life and love, streaming down from above, be channeled *through* me, blessing *me* on its way to blessing *others*. Instead of feeling like life's dartboard, I could choose to be God's pipeline.

Choosing to be God's pipeline, however, meant that I must be willing to reverse my old reactions and find new ways of responding to difficult situations as they arose. By now I was more than willing, but the question was this: next time I was faced with one of those annoying predicaments of life, exactly what was I to do, or think, or say, *instead of complaining?*

Instinctively I reached for pen and paper, and I was amazed at the guidelines that began to flow from my pen. In the light of all that the Lord had shown me minutes before, I was coming up with a "pattern for predicaments" (that's the name I later gave it), a pattern of new responses that was meant to be exercised *right in the middle of a predicament.* Here is the pattern, almost exactly as I recorded it that day:

> 1. **Remember** that God anticipated this predicament, and He already knows what He intends to do;
> 2. **Believe** that God has a solution, provision, deliverance, or gift of wisdom to match this and every predicament.
> 3. **Pray** as a first resort, declaring faith in God and His intentions—not faith in faith, but faith in God.
> 4. **Wait** with positive expectancy and availability, making God responsible to work out His intentions in the predicament, for He wants this responsibility.
> 5. **Praise Him** before He acts, for He will certainly be praised afterwards.

That evening I attended a small ladies' meeting in my church. Somewhere I had read that if a person wants to give up smoking or lose weight, it's a good idea to tell a few friends about it so that one must carry it out or else lose face. With that in mind, during our sharing time I told the ladies of my decision to give up the luxury of complaint and why. I also shared my decision with one or two ladies in our neighborhood Bible study. I knew that all these friends would be watching me like hawks and asking for progress reports whenever they saw me. Thus another experiment was launched, and none too soon, for the very next day I would be facing a most annoying predicament.

Marion and Becky, two good friends of mine from nearby Wheaton, had been in touch with me a few days earlier. Together we had agreed to have a surprise birthday coffee at my house for Linda, a mutual friend of ours. Linda had been in and out of the hospital for many months and was in need of all the love and support we could give her. It was going to be just the four of us and Marion would be driving them to my house at about one o'clock that day. During the morning I was going to bake a birthday cake and give it the works—candles and all.

But alas, that part of the plan wasn't to be. First one intrusion and then another kept me from getting the cake mixed. Finally time ran out completely as I answered a distress call from one of my neighbors. But did I complain? No, not yet, for I still hadn't reached the point of having my back against the wall. For one thing, I knew I could dash to the local bakery if necessary, buy a ready-made birthday cake, and get it home before the others arrived. By now this step was indeed necessary. *Ah well,* I assured myself, *spending half the morning being a good Samaritan is more important than baking a cake. And anyway, it's the thought that counts.*

And so, feeling rushed but not downhearted, I hopped into my car and headed for town, a couple of miles away. I still felt on top of things, plus the Lord was with me, for the entire day had been devoted to Him and to others. The fleeting memory of my car stalling a couple of days earlier didn't disturb me. The Lord knew I didn't have time for that today. He also knew that Bill was out of town.

Wait a minute . . . is this engine "missing" on me? I thought to myself, listening carefully as I drove along, *Or did I only imagine it?* I hadn't! The car began to sputter, cough, and jerk so that I barely managed to get it over to the curb before it gave one last shudder and died. Being careful not to flood it, I nonetheless failed in every effort to restart it. Reality finally hit me. This car wasn't going anywhere, at least not in time to get me to the bakery and home again before the others arrived.

With my back firmly against the wall, my first impulse was to complain—loudly! There was a time when that first impulse would have been my only option and the one I certainly would have given in to. Within seconds I would have been in the middle of a pity party and indulging myself to the hilt. But now I had an alternative, and I knew what it was—God's magnificent alternative, which had taught me to be dead to the impulse of self and alive to the impulse of the Spirit. That meant I now had a choice in such predicaments as this—either to limit God by complaining or to let God be God by yielding to Him. And He wasn't slow to remind me that yielding to Him meant putting that new "pattern for predicaments" to the test.

"Okay, Lord," I began with a stressful sigh, "this seems to be the moment you've been preparing me for. So here goes." The decision not to get carried away with my usual complaining but to turn around and do something else instead was like swimming against the tide. But swim against it I did. First I reminded myself that the Lord had seen this predicament coming and knew what He wanted to do. Then I affirmed that He had either a solution or a provision or a deliverance or a gift of wisdom for me that would match this problem suitably. Trying to sound bold, I then declared my faith in Him and His power to act, making sure that my faith was in Him and not in faith itself, feeble as my faith at the moment felt.

"Well, Lord," I said finally, "it's over to you now. And I already praise you for what you're going to do, before you do it!" In an effort to wait expectantly rather than anxiously, I began to mull over a few memorized Scriptures, such as, "Be still and know that I am God," and "Stand still and see the salvation of the Lord."

Presently a car crept past mine and pulled over to the curb in front of me. A well-dressed man got out and came over to where I sat. Supposing that he only wanted to ask for directions, I rolled my car window down, but only a few inches.

"You got car trouble, lady?" he asked. How he knew I was parked there because my car wouldn't start was a mystery to me.

"Yes, I really don't know what's wrong with it," I replied. "I barely got it to the curb before it died on me."

"I see," he said, almost as if my problem were his to solve. "If you'll pull the latch for the hood, I'll be glad to have a look at the engine."

While he disappeared behind the raised hood, I stayed put in the car, keeping all doors locked. I didn't know this man from Adam, and I wasn't about to be taken in by charm. On the other hand, he just might be God's answer to my predicament. With one eye on the car clock, I prayed earnestly that he might be able to solve the problem and solve it quickly, as time was running out.

Pretty soon he slammed the hood back into place and, wiping grease off his fingers with his handkerchief, he walked back to where I sat. "Well, I'm afraid this car isn't going to start."

Thanks a million! I thought inwardly with a hint of sarcasm. *I hardly needed you to tell me that!* Next thing I knew I was pouring out my tale of woe, telling him how much I had counted on my car to get me to the local bakery where I was going to buy a birthday cake for some friends who were due to arrive at my house shortly. I knew my voice was communicating desperation, but not for one moment did I expect or him to offer anything but a bit of sympathy.

"Look," he suggested, "I'll be glad to take you to the bakery and then drop you off at your home. You can leave your car here and deal with it later."

Warning signals started flashing in my mind and obviously registered in my eyes, letting him know that I wasn't about to get into a car with a strange man. "Oh, I'm sorry, I don't blame you for being cautious," he said with a fatherly smile on his face, "but you're safe with me." Producing a piece of identification, he went on to say, "You see, I'm a plainclothes policeman. You can take a look at the instruments in my car for further proof, if you wish."

I ventured out, and sure enough, everything I could imagine a police car having was there. "So hop in," he said, "we'll get you home with that cake in no time."

No longer afraid of him, instead I now held him in awe. A policeman, I reasoned, has more important things to do than to chauffeur a disorganized woman to the bakery to buy a cake! As someone who always hated putting people out, I felt this was simply too much to ask, and I told him so.

"I'm more than glad to be of service to you," he insisted. "After all, what are policemen for?"

But I kept saying things like, "Oh no, I couldn't possibly let you use your valuable time dealing with such an insignificant problem as mine."

"What will you do, then?" he asked, obviously sincere in his concern over my so-called insignificant problem.

"Well . . . er . . . I've just spotted a public phone. I'll go over there and call my next-door neighbor. I'm sure she'll be able to come in her car to help me out."

"Well, all right then," he said with a shrug of his shoulders, obviously giving up on me, "have it your way." Then he turned, got in his car, and drove away.

Before he was out of sight, I knew I had done the wrong thing. His last words, "Have it *your* way," hit me between the eyes. My way was now all I had left, and it was up to me to see it through.

I ran over to the phone booth, called Bev, and begged her to bail me out, and fast. Though swamped with the responsibilities of eight children, an aged, live-in mother-in-law, and a huge house, she was willing to pull herself away to come to my aid. She zoomed me to the bakery and back home again with about three minutes to spare, during which time I managed to sling a few plates on the table before breathlessly opening the door to my friends from Wheaton.

Good-hearted as Bev had been and grateful as I was for her help, she and I both knew she had been the wrong person for the task. The right person had been that policeman, for he had been *sent* to me, from where I didn't know. All I knew was, I had put the pattern to the test, God had sent someone to help, and I had turned that help away—and merely because I hadn't wanted to put that someone out. Yet how much more I had put Bev out!

God's rebuke in my heart was a serious one, but it was a loving rebuke and certainly was corrective in effect, which is all He ever wants from our failures. Never again, at least not knowingly, would I refuse God's provision. As far as complaining was concerned, I knew I still was capable of it, but never again would I be able to indulge myself in that way with a clear conscience. In fact, I found it pretty difficult to put God to the test and complain at the same time.

Yes, God was changing me into a more positive person, but not the sort who forever "accentuates the positive and eliminates the negative," as one old popular song used to instruct us to do. It is quite true, of course, that a positive attitude is a lot easier to live with than a negative one. Just ask my family! But the sort of positiveness God was building into me was a positiveness concerning *Him,* not *me.* I wasn't going around knocking over disheartened people with platitudes like, "You can if you think you can," or "God helps those who help themselves." Rather, I was proving through personal experience that God can when you know you can't, that God helps those who can't help themselves. In other words, I was beginning to "let life happen *through* me"— God's life, and not only His life, but His power as well.

I couldn't help marveling whenever I sensed God's power flowing in and through me as a weak human vessel. Presumably He didn't mind making use of a humble pipeline, as long as it was clean and open at both ends. As a result, prayers were being answered, acts of God were taking place, people in need were being helped, small deeds performed in faith were effective. And through it all, a long-standing concern of mine was being put to rest, a concern that went back to my first year at Taylor University.

In some of my biblical studies, I had had the disturbing feeling that I was understanding the Bible only on an academic level rather than on a spiritual level, yet I felt powerless to do anything about it. When I sought the counsel of one of my professors, he questioned me about my Christian experience and then decided that he too was unable to help me.

During the following summer I worked as a volunteer with a gospel mission in the heart of the Kentucky mountains. In that remote, backwoods environment, I began to experience what can only be called a "homesickness" for Christ. Though I had received Him into my life and had yielded my all to Him, I wanted more—more of Christ. I concluded that the only way I could have more of Him was to go to heaven. Since my death didn't appear to be imminent, I could only hope and pray that Christ's return might take place *now* so that I could be taken home with Him. Often I would stop along some mountain pathway, look up into the clouds, and plead, "Oh Lord, it seems selfish of me to think you would come back to earth just because I ask you to, but I can't bear it unless I find a way to be closer to you. If it's possible, please come back today and take me home with you!"

Late one night, in fact it was my last night in the Kentucky mountains, the fire of the Holy Spirit became real as I prayed. I was speechless as He purged me and burned the love of Christ into my inner being. The next day, I traveled back to my home in Michigan. A few weeks later when I returned to Taylor and resumed my biblical studies, I realized that things were different, that now I was understanding the Scriptures with a new heart and mind, just as I had longed to do.

Then came the passing of years. During those desert years in Switzerland, my one secret comfort was the *memory* of my Kentucky experience. At the same time, I was reminded that one shouldn't live off past experiences. Perhaps I should be seeking another such experience, I thought, to restore the love and power of God within me. And so, during the early days of my healing, I sought God's will in this matter. Within a short time I received His answer as I came across 1 John 2:27: "As for you, the anointing you received from him remains in you. . . . But as his anointing teaches you about all things and as that anointing is real, not counterfeit—just as it has taught you, *remain in him*" (NIV).

From that day, I accepted that my anointing was still intact, waiting only to be released at some point in my healing process. Now I had reached that point. Just as my spiritual anointing had remained in me, now I was learning to remain in Him, to live and move and have my being in Him. God's magnificent alternative had seen to that, and as a result, His power was being released in me.

The Divine Intruder

10 It was Bill's day off, and he and I were quietly enjoying each other's company and relaxing. As we walked and then caught up on our reading together, two of our favorite shared pastimes, I sensed that Bill wanted to talk about something, something of importance to both of us.

About mid-afternoon he took me by the hand and led me to the sofa where we could sit together comfortably. "Joanie . . ." he began cautiously, but not wasting words, "I don't know how you're going to feel about this, but for some time now I've felt God calling us back overseas, perhaps this time to live in England to avoid another language change in the girls' education." Bill knew how revolutionary these last couple of years had been in my own life, and he was being careful not to bring up this idea in a pushy, unfeeling way. For all he knew, perhaps I was secretly hoping we would end up staying in the States permanently.

Reaching out to squeeze his hand, I was pleased to say, "You've got nothing to worry about, Bill. For some time now I've sensed our time in the U.S. drawing to a close, but I decided to wait and see if we both felt the same. Praise the Lord, we do!"

Bill was overjoyed to find that God had been preparing the two of us for this new direction. Before moving ahead on it, however, we knew we must talk it over with Tina and Heidi and listen carefully to their response. Such a move was going to affect them profoundly, and we wished to do nothing against their wills. In fact, Bill and I believed that their response would be a way of testing God's will; if this plan was of Him, then they would be prepared for it just as we had been. If not, we would have to think and pray again.

By now Tina was sweet sixteen and never been kissed (well, nearly never) and Heidi was nine with talking brown eyes. How would these two developing young girls feel about leaving America and adjusting yet again to foreign schools? As Bill shared our thoughts with them, we both hoped they at least might be open to the idea. But not in our wildest imagination had we expected to see them jumping up and down in the middle of the room, clapping their hands and hugging each other. And so, as quickly and as joyously as that, a whole new future for our family was set, a future that none of us, at this point, could have predicted.

From that moment, the wheels of change began to turn rapidly. Perhaps the most major change was Bill's tough decision to leave Youth for Christ. Alongside his work at our Wheaton headquarters, he had been working on a degree in modern missions at Wheaton College. Through these studies, Bill had become burdened to see "saturation evangelism" taking place in parts of Europe, a method whereby a host of laypeople from local churches would be mobilized and trained to be effective witnesses throughout their communities. Getting involved in this type of ministry, of course, would take us well beyond the specialized youth ministry in which we so far had been involved. Quite apart from that, we reasoned, perhaps it was time we got out of youth work anyway (we were pushing forty) and cleared the way for a younger breed of workers. In light of all that, Bill began to set up an organization of our own—nothing large, just an adequate framework to help Bill accomplish what he now felt led to do. Together with our newly appointed board of directors, we agreed that the name of our new organization should be "Operation Concern."

By August of 1972, roughly three years after our arrival in the U.S., our move to England was imminent. As barrels, boxes, and trunks were being packed, countless good-byes were being said. On our last Sunday in West Chicago, as we drove into our driveway after Sunday morning services, we were intercepted and hustled off to a surprise farewell party hosted by our neighbors. They and their families had gathered together in someone's backyard and were standing in a line, waiting for us to pass by each one to receive a warm handshake or some expression of appreciation or just a hug laced with tears. As if that were not enough, at the end of the line we were presented with an envelope containing a generous check for our new work. And then we all shared food together, wonderful West Chicago recipes prepared by our wonderful West Chicago friends, many of them ladies from our Bible study. These ladies, more than all the others, knew who they were saying good-bye to—to a woman who had arrived in human weakness and was leaving in spiritual strength. Between those two points had been a drama, theirs and mine, in which we'd all had parts to play. But the lead part had been the Lord's. Our weekly meetings with Him around our oval table meant that none of us would ever be the same.

Days later we closed the door to our house for the last time. I had anticipated this moment and had decided that, since the best was yet before us, I wouldn't so much as look back over my shoulder. I was going to be a forward-looking person from now on. At O'Hare airport we boarded a jumbo jet, and off we flew into a brand new chapter of our lives, a chapter yet unwritten.

Moving to Reading, England, was like coming home. Soon all the basics were intact—a cozy house in which to live, a warm, friendly church in which to worship and grow, and good schools into which our girls were happily settled. Bill was already zigzagging between England and Europe, mostly to Finland, where he was laying the groundwork for his first interchurch "mobilization project."

At last I was the happiest American woman on the face of the earth. To borrow some words from a friend of mine, "I felt as if I had joy running through my veins, rather than blood," and this joy was longing to be given away by the gallon. As the months went by, all I could think of were those dropouts and drug addicts we were reading so much about in the newspapers, many of them in prison for one reason or another. I longed to get into those prisons and move from cell to cell to announce to each inmate: "You can be free without ever leaving your cell. Jesus can set you free inside yourself." (How well I knew it.) But since that wasn't possible, I collected every newspaper article I could find that reported the misdemeanors of young addicts and prayed for them by name, if given. I asked God to do what I couldn't do, to move from cell to cell and somehow to alert them to His reality and great love. Though we had taken ourselves out of the youth ministry, apparently the youth ministry hadn't been taken out of us, certainly not out of me. Not only that, I couldn't seem to forget those words that the Lord had given me earlier on: "if I can trust you, I will entrust you."

Now that our girls were getting older, the four of us often had the pleasure of engaging in adult conversations as a family. One time between Bill's travels, we found ourselves talking about needy people and the value of having an open home. Presently we sensed the Lord using our conversation to place a serious challenge before our entire family, and the challenge was this: would we be willing to let the Lord use our home, our time, our energies, our entire resources whenever He wished, however He wished, and with whomever He wished—no strings attached?

I remember thinking to myself rather defensively, *I thought we already* did *have an open home!* But on second thought, I knew I preferred that people came when invited, I preferred that they came when the house was tidy and when there was plenty of food on hand, and I certainly preferred that people came when it was convenient for *me*. No, what I had called an open home definitely had a lot of strings attached to it.

Before ending our conversation, we all agreed to cut all strings and to do our part in making ours a more open home for the Lord to use, whatever the cost. After sealing our agreement by prayer, we got up and went about our busy ways, little knowing how crucial this family commitment would prove to be later on.

One beautiful spring morning about eighteen months after we had arrived in Reading, I had the sudden urge to paint Heidi's bedroom, something I had considered doing for some time. With gusto I pulled down the curtains, cleared away cobwebs, and single-handedly shoved heavy things out of her room. With paint and brushes ready, I suddenly remembered that I hadn't had my coffee break with the Lord. After pouring coffee, I flopped down in an easy chair with my Bible on my lap. Before I even had a chance to open its pages, the Spirit of God spoke within my spirit in a tone of strong authority: *"I'm about to give you and Bill a totally new work to do,"* He said, *"but unless you trust me for it, I can't give it to you."*

Tears began to rise from deep within me and streamed down my face, down my sweater, and into my hands. I immediately knew what the Lord meant when He spoke of our need to trust Him. By now Bill had so many commitments in Finland, he practically lived there. All his efforts to get some full-time assistance had been unsuccessful, and we were wringing our hands in frustration, wondering how in the world all these commitments were going to be met. In the face of all this, the Lord seemed to be saying, *"Be still, cease striving. I've got something new I want you to do, but unless you stop wringing your hands, I can't give it to you."*

Fortunately, Bill was home at the time. After mopping up my tears, I went up to his study where he was dictating letters and shared this word from the Lord with him. Bill listened with interest, pondered it for a moment, and then said, "Let's pray about it." So we did. Mysterious as it all seemed, we could do nothing else but hand it over to the Lord. After that we could only wait and see.

After our chat, I had *every* intention of getting into my painting project. Instead I decided to stretch out on our bed, as I felt decidedly unwell all of a sudden. For over a week I continued to feel unwell and was able to eat very little except for cups of broth or tea. *This is just super,* I thought to myself, my old complaining instinct coming to the fore. *God tells me He's going to give us a new work to do, and here I am, too weak to do it!*

After several more days of not getting any better, I finally crawled out of bed, got dressed, and acted as if I were well, for Bill and I each had a meeting we were to speak at down in Dorset—Bill at Moorland's Bible College and I at a ladies' meeting. By now I was running on God's strength alone, for I was still unable to eat more than a few morsels of food. But we got to Bournemouth, got through our meetings, and then, none too soon for my liking, were driving back to Reading again. On top of my condition of weakness, we had the aggravation of car trouble along the way, making the sight of home all the more welcome at the end of our journey.

As we came into the house, the telephone was ringing, and I rushed over to answer it. "Ah, Joanie," the voice at the other end said with a sigh of relief, "I've got through to you at last!" It was Ernie, an elderly gentleman from our church, a godly man who was partially disabled and was often in need of a ride from church members in order to get places.

"Here's my situation," he went on to explain, "I've got two tickets in my hand—one for me and one for a driver.

They're for the annual concert of the London Emmanuel Choir taking place tonight at Central Hall, Westminster. You see, Joanie, last year I was taken to their concert, and I've been dreaming ever since of going back. So far I've not been able to find a driver, and you're my last resort. I wonder, could either you or Bill help me out?".

"I'm so sorry, Ernie," I replied, hoping that my excuse sounded real, "but our car has given us considerable trouble today, and we dare not take it on the road again until it's been repaired."

Ernie was clearly heartbroken, for his year-long dream was now out of the question, and he knew it. But he rallied quickly by proposing something else. "Look, Joanie, I can't bear to see these two tickets lying here unused. Why don't you and Bill come and collect them and go to the concert yourselves? Just because I can't go by train doesn't mean you can't! I ask just one favor. If you do go, perhaps you'd be good enough to bring back one of their LPs for me."

I covered the mouthpiece of the phone momentarily to ask what Bill thought, hoping he'd make it easy for me by saying he'd rather not go. Instead, with his nose already in the evening newspaper, he diplomatically said, "I'll leave it up to you, Joanie. If you want to go, we will, and if you don't, we won't." I definitely didn't feel like going, so speaking again to Ernie I said, "I'm awfully sorry, but I've been under the weather for a number of days now, and I think it would be best if I stayed in tonight. Thanks anyway, Ernie." And with that we hung up.

No sooner had I put the phone down, than I had a compelling sense that I should reverse my decision. When a husband tells a wife she can do as she pleases, she feels free to do exactly that, even if it means changing her mind. Calling Ernie straight back, I informed him, to his great delight, that Bill would come along shortly to pick up the tickets. In the meantime, I made supper for Bill and the girls.

Since I still couldn't bear to eat, I put a hastily made ham sandwich into a plastic bag and stuck it into my handbag, just in case I suddenly got healthy in the middle of the concert. Then Bill and I caught a bus to Reading Station, hurriedly bought tickets to Paddington Station, and ran all the way up to platform 5, where a train was about ready to leave. In fact, we barely got in before the door was closed behind us and the train began to move.

Feeling weaker and wearier than ever, I sank down into the seat next to Bill, asking myself, *Why on earth am I doing this? I want to be home, relaxing in front of the TV and having an early night.* I didn't expect a response to my musing, of course, and I certainly didn't expect what happened next. In an instant, it was as if God's invisible hand rolled back the ceiling of the train, rolled back the heavy clouds, and opened the windows of heaven over me, pouring something overwhelming into me, more and more of it until I was filled to overflowing. I recognized what it was, almost as if it came with a label on it. It was the compassion of Christ—not my compassion, but *His,* coming down from above and traveling with us into London. Talk about life happening *through* me!

I nudged Bill—I couldn't help myself—and said, "Wow, have you ever been so filled with the compassion of Christ that you hardly knew what to do with it?" I can't recall what Bill said in return, but we began discussing the compassion of Christ, reminding ourselves of needy ones He had met during the course of His earthly life. We spoke particularly of the immediacy with which He responded to people who reached out to Him.

In no time at all we were in London and on a subway train heading for Westminster. The train was jammed with people, many of them commuters and shoppers heading for home, so at first there were no available seats. Constantly being jerked and pressed against other warm bodies, I kept scanning the train for signs of someone in need of this compassion, which by now was churning around inside me, desperate for an outlet. But oddly enough, everyone within sight looked remarkably content and peaceful. After a few stops the crowds began to thin out, and Bill and I took seats opposite one another next to a window.

Before long the person seated next to me got off, and at the same time a young man boarded at the other end of the train. He was dressed in grubby looking jeans, his hair was long and greasy, and he had a brown cloth bag hanging on a strap from one shoulder. Once inside, he glanced up and down the train, looking for a place to sit down. Seeing the empty seat next to me, he staggered up the aisle and dropped himself into the seat, practically falling into my lap. The minute he sat down, I felt Christ's compassion move out like an electric current toward this young man, identifying him as the one He had been waiting for.

He began counting a few coins in his hand, but because he was suffering from the effect of drugs, they slipped out of his hand and fell to the floor, rolling in all directions. Without a moment's thought, I promptly gathered them up and pressed them into his hand again with the words, "You'd better put this change in your pocket, or you're going to lose it." This he attempted to do, straining to get his hand into the pocket of his skintight jeans. Once successful, he leaned over to me, and in blurred speech he asked, "Got any bread?"

What a time for me to have one of my naive moments. When he said "bread," I thought of only one sort, and I knew I had it—my ham sandwich! As I reached into my handbag, I was thinking, *Amazing, this is the only time I've ever carried a sandwich on the train, and here's someone asking for it!* Then the thought came to me, *This fellow needs more than a sandwich, he needs the Bread of Life.* So I fished around in my bag further until I came up with a gospel tract. Laying it on top of the sandwich, I handed both over to him with a smile. Though he accepted them, I noticed he seemed surprised—surprised, I assumed, at getting exactly what he had asked for.

Now I was the surprised one, for I was expecting to have the satisfaction of seeing him eat the sandwich hungrily. Instead, he tucked it into his cloth bag, but interestingly enough, he kept the leaflet in his hand and began looking through it. All of a sudden I heard myself saying, "You're on drugs, aren't you." Not a very inspiring opener, but it got a response. "Yeah . . ." he answered slowly, "I've been on drugs for a long time, and I'm afraid I'm going to die."

If he wasn't hungry for a ham sandwich, he was obviously hungry for life. "Tell me," I responded, "hasn't anyone ever told you about Jesus?"

Until that moment, I hadn't seen his face, for his head and his long hair were constantly drooping downwards, obscuring his face. But now he raised his head. Looking at me with hazy eyes, he said with sadness, "Jesus? I pray to Him every day, but help doesn't come."

Without a moment's forethought, I answered, "Well, thank God, He's answering your prayers, for *we* can help you!" Suddenly I felt completely out of my depth. Inside myself I did a hasty mental review of drug-related books I had read like *The Cross and the Switchblade* and *Run, Baby, Run,* desperate to find some clue as to how we might help this young man. But my mind drew a blank. I looked across at Bill for the first time, hoping for a bit of help or encouragement; all he gave me were a few subtle eye signals telling me to be careful.

But there was no time to worry or wonder further, for next thing I knew, this young man was asking me for the one sort of help I *could* have given him, but which hadn't occurred to me. "Would you pray for me?" he asked simply.

"We would love to pray for you," I answered, thinking that we might have to wait until we got home later that evening. "Would you pray for me by name?" he asked further. "Oh, yes," I said, deeply touched, "that's exactly how we'd like to pray for you. What is your name?"

He asked for pen and paper so that he could jot it down for me, but his hands were too unsteady to write, so he asked me to do it for him. Derek Paisley was his name, and his address for the moment was Teak Ward at the Springfield Hospital in Tooting. Derek explained that he was in the hospital for the sixth time for a "detox." They had put him in a locked ward to keep him from all outside contact, but as usual, he had grown uptight, had conned the nurse about a fake phone call, and once out of the ward, had slipped out of the hospital and back to the "Dilly" for a new supply of drugs. "Now look at me," he said in a despairing voice, "I know I'm going to die!"

Just then the train jerked to a stop. It wasn't our stop, but he thought it was. Wanting to give me a fond farewell, he leaned toward me and put his arms around me. "We're not getting off just yet," I said, hoping he'd realize by the "we" that I was not alone. "But since you're leaning on me, let me pray for you right now." "Yes, please," he answered.

With his ear in the region of my mouth and with other passengers (not to mention Bill) watching wide-eyed, I prayed the compassion of Christ into that ear. I prayed for the Lord to save him and to deliver him, not only from drugs but from all sin, and to give him new life and hope.

The next stop was ours. As Bill and I stood up, we both urged Derek to go straight back to the hospital, where we promised to write to him. Then we got off the train and stood to wave as the train began moving out. As he waved back and smiled, I saw in his eyes something that wasn't there the first time I looked into them. It was hope—the beautiful hope of Christ.

Off we went to Central Hall, *minus* my ham sandwich, where I sat and wept throughout the entire performance. I couldn't help but feeling emotional. In fact, each in our own way, Bill and I both felt emotional as we listened to one gospel song after another proclaiming the love of Jesus. Each song seemed a heartrending reminder that somewhere out there on the streets of London was a young man named Derek who had been sought and found by that love. And no less amazing, He had chosen to channel His love through ordinary, unsuspecting, weak, and naive people like ourselves.

Overnight my strength and my appetite returned. Had my weakness been God's intention, I wondered? Was I possibly a contemporary example of what Paul wrote about in 1 Corinthians 1:27, that God *chooses* the foolish things of the world (even a naive woman carrying a ham sandwich?) that He *chooses* the weak things of the world (common clay vessels like ourselves bearing the compassion of Christ?). I believed this to be so, and I began to feel grateful, sincerely grateful, for my foolishness and my weakness, for it meant that there was only one explanation for what had happened, and that explanation was *God.*

The day after meeting Derek, Bill and I sent a letter to him at the hospital, and we immediately received a reply back. So he had gone back as we had urged him to! In his letter he expressed his desire to know more about God and to have a Bible of his own. Bill and I wasted no time before visiting him in the hospital, where we also presented him with a Bible. As he took it into his hands, thanking us profusely, we couldn't help noticing the sense of reverence with which he handled it. After opening and reopening it a number of times, he held it to his chest for a moment and simply beamed at us.

In due course, at Derek's request, we were able to arrange for him to leave the hospital to enter a rehabilitation program. *What a wonderful outcome to a wonderful encounter,* we thought to ourselves with deep satisfaction. After a few days we called the center, eager to find out how well Derek was getting along. To our shock, they hardly remembered who we were talking about. Derek had left soon after he had arrived, and they had no idea where he was.

No idea where he was? We found this news almost unbearable. In a very painful way we were discovering how deeply we already loved him. They may as well have told us that one of our daughters was missing, so great was our sorrow.

Bill and I slept very fitfully that night. Over our early morning cup of tea, Bill announced with a sound of resolution in his voice, "Well, I know what I'm going to do today. I'm going to London to look for Derek."

"You're going to do *what?*" I asked, hardly believing my ears. With faith as flat as a pancake, I questioned Bill further, "How on earth do you expect to find one person in the midst of millions? Isn't that a bit like hunting for a needle in a haystack?"

"I'll tell you how I expect to do it," Bill replied, obviously having thought it through long before this conversation. "You're going to find a prayer partner and pray together that I'll be able to find him. And when I have, I'll call you from London so that you can start praising the Lord. And by the way," he went on, "I plan to have a partner, too. I'm going to ask Brian to come with me." Brian was an outgoing, people-loving young man who loved being part of the action in our lives.

I felt thoroughly ashamed of myself but so proud of Bill. Then he told me that all night he had dreamed that he was in London looking for Derek and that somewhere in it all there was a dark-skinned man. What it all meant, he didn't know. But one thing he did know, in dependence on the Lord, he was going to London!

After Bill and Brian had set off for the big city, dressed as casually as possible in blue jeans and T-shirts, with crosses on chains hanging from their necks, my friend Sheila, who had the day off, came over, and we began to talk and pray. It's hard to say if I had any real faith or not as we prayed. All I know is, I nearly fell over with surprise and joy when the telephone rang that afternoon and I heard Bill saying, "Hi, Joanie. Guess who I've got standing next to me. That's right, Derek. And he sends his love to you." Needless to say, Sheila and I started to praise the Lord together, still hardly believing the good news that Derek had been found.

Later Bill filled us in on the story. The first detail of the episode stemmed from our original encounter with Derek on the subway. While Bill had sat watching the unfolding drama taking place between Derek and me, he was doing something that he was very good at—*listening*. At some point, he heard Derek mention Portobello Road, a detail I had missed entirely, but Bill had stored away in his memory for future reference. So when he and Brian went to London, they headed for Portobello Road. They spent hours walking up and down this fascinating road, once a posh area filled with antique shops, but fast becoming a run-down center for drug users. They stopped everyone they met and asked if they knew Derek Paisley. They went into every shop, into every pub, asking the same. Nobody seemed to recognize the name, but Bill and Brian refused to give up. Finally one man, speaking a bit guardedly out of fear that Bill and Brian might be a couple of "narcs," gave the first tip-off that finally led them to a nearby "squat," where they found not only Derek, but a small group of other addicts, all trying to kick the habit together. In keeping with Bill's dream, their leader was a big, friendly black man, a forty-five-year-old Nigerian named Johnny who had kicked the habit in prison and was now trying to help others do the same. But none of them, including Derek, seemed to be making much progress. In fact, several weeks after Bill found Derek, he was kicked out of the squat and had nowhere to go.

Nowhere to go . . . nowhere to go. Was this God speaking to us? Was He now taking us at our word when our family promised to let Him use our home, our time, our energies, our resources whenever He wished, however He wished, and with whomever He wished, no strings attached? The four of us got together and unanimously agreed that He was. A few hours later, after a flying trip to and from London, Bill and I had a twenty-three-year-old son living in our home, who in turn became an adored brother to Tina and Heidi. Whether we chose to be or not (and we hadn't), we were back in youth work again.

As I pondered all this, I remembered that C. S. Lewis had once referred to God as "the divine intruder." Through an unexpected encounter on the London subway, Bill and I had experienced God as an intruder. But one thing I had learned—living in dependence on Him will always give God His rightful freedom to intrude, a freedom I had seen Him take time and again in small, everyday ways. This time He had intruded in a big way, but it wouldn't be long until we realized that this divine intrusion spelled the difference between a ministry based on good plans and a ministry based on God's purposes. Or as King Solomon put it in one of his proverbs, "Many are the plans in a man's heart, but it is the LORD's purpose that prevails," (Prov. 19:21 NIV).

No Apology Needed

11   "Well, whatever it is you people have got, I want it," Derek announced the day he arrived in our home. We were finding out he always had a way of getting straight to the point.

"I know it has to do with Jesus Christ," he continued, interspersing his comments with sips from a mug of tea, "but quite honestly, all I know about Jesus Christ is . . . well . . . you know . . . just Jesus Christ." His voice trailed off at that point but we got his meaning. It was his way of saying that until now, Jesus Christ was little more than a name, possibly a name to swear by.

It was Saturday afternoon, and we had just finished a hearty meal of burgers and fries around the kitchen table before moving into the living room with our mugs of tea. We were all sitting comfortably, Tina and Heidi on the floor and Derek at one end of the couch, which, from that day onwards, was reserved as "Derek's place." This became the setting for a discussion that lasted for three days.

During those remarkable days the five of us seemed to do little else but sit around drinking tea and talking, mostly about this Jesus Christ whom Derek was so eager to know. Through our discussions we discovered that Derek was intelligent, logical, and articulate. His questions were rational and real. They were questions that we were able to answer out of the Bible, giving us a natural opportunity to share the good news of Jesus with him.

By the third day Derek finally reached his saturation point. "I guess there's nothing more to discuss," he said, trying to sum things up. "I know that everything you've told me about Jesus is true. I also know that I'm a sinner and that I need God's forgiveness, lots of it. But that's where I've got a real problem."

Getting straight to the point once again, he looked us in the eye and said, "It seems to me that it would be pretty cheap of me to come to God after all I've done and say to Him, 'Well, God, how about forgiving me now?' It would be different," he explained candidly, "if I could say that I hadn't known any better when I did the things that I did. But I can't say that. I knew that the things I did were wrong, not just after I did them, but as I was doing them."

Then he reeled off a number of things he had done that he knew at the time to be sins, such as stealing from his parents to get money for drugs and being aggressive with his brothers because of the effect drugs were having on him. Most serious of all, he told us about his unsuccessful marriage to his teenage girlfriend, Connie, and the tragic death of their baby daughter. "That little baby needn't have died," Derek said with sorrow and pain written across his face. "She died only because Connie and I were so busy using drugs that when she developed a minor illness, we neglected to get her the medical attention she needed and complications set in. So you see what I mean?" he finished off. "It would be cheap of me to come to God after all that and simply ask Him to forgive me."

Derek didn't know it, but he had just created for himself an ideal opportunity to find out what the word *gospel* really means.

"Derek," we responded with excitement in our hearts, "have we ever got good news for you!" Then Bill and I in turn sought to make that good news clear. Drawing his attention to Christ's death, we explained that on the cross *Jesus* had been punished *instead of Derek* for the very sins that he had just described. As best we could, with the Holy Spirit helping us, we explained that as Jesus hung on the cross, suffering to the point of shedding His blood, He was accomplishing something on our behalf. He was atoning for our sins and was intercepting God's wrath, which by all rights should have fallen on us. Now, God can forgive our sins without overlooking them, for they have been dealt with fully in Jesus. As we shared, we longed that Derek would begin to see God's forgiveness as a free gift, a gift that would not be cheapened by his grateful acceptance of it.

"So you see, Derek," Bill said, now appealing to his fine reasoning powers, "forgiveness for sin isn't something that can be deserved. If we could deserve it, then surely we wouldn't need it!" Derek laughed over the sheer logic of Bill's words. "But the fact is," Bill went on, "forgiveness is something we all need—not just you, but all of us in this room and everyone in the world. Jesus loves you and *wants* to forgive you, Derek. His death tells you *how much* He loves you and *how much* He wants to forgive you."

Derek was getting the message. This was evidenced by his tear-filled eyes but even more by the revealing words that spontaneously came out of his mouth. "Looking at it like that," Derek pondered thoughtfully, "what a terrible waste of all that Jesus did on the cross if I didn't receive my forgiveness."

What could anyone add to such a revelation as that? It seemed he already knew a lot about making full use of Calvary. By then it was time to go to bed, time to shut up and let God do the rest.

The next morning as I was cooking breakfast, Derek came into the kitchen and hovered around the stove as I watched over the eggs, trying to get them just right. With spatula in hand I thought to myself, *He wants to tell me something.* Presently he said, "Er, Joanie . . . I thought you might like to know . . . last night up in my room I asked Jesus to come into my life . . . and I received my forgiveness."

This was like Christmas, New Year, and a birthday all rolled into one. I felt like tossing and turning those eggs high in the air like pancakes! "Oh, Derek!" I exclaimed, suffering a complete loss of words. With my one free arm I reached out and gave him a hug like the one he had given me on the London subway, hoping that a hug said it all. Then he dashed off to tell Bill.

That evening when we had our usual family prayers around our supper table I thought to myself, *One of these days—we won't pressure him—perhaps Derek can be encouraged to join us in our family prayers.* But before our prayers were finished, we found out that Derek didn't need our encouragement. Taking quick advantage of a gap between prayers, he offered a beautiful prayer of thanksgiving to God for finding him and for giving him the gift of forgiveness.

A bit later on, Bill and Derek went to visit Ernie, that godly man from our church who had been so disappointed over not being able to go to hear the London Emmanuel Choir. His sadness had been turned to joy, of course, when we told him the next day how God had used his disappointment to set off a whole chain of events. Ernie was in a nursing home by then and was very frail. Meeting Derek and hearing him say, "Thank you, Ernie, for being in the right place at the right time," was possibly one of his last joys before slipping away to glory not long after.

In the meantime, Derek was going through many ups and downs, and we with him. Pressure would build up; he would "split" and run off to London to "score drugs," overdose, and end up in the emergency room for a stomach pump. Then the emergency room would call us, and we would drive to London to bring him home again. Every time this happened our entire family died a thousand deaths as we waited in agony to hear whether our beloved Derek was dead or alive.

These ups and downs were teaching us that Derek not only had a lot to learn from us, we also had plenty to learn from him. Bill and I knew practically nothing about drugs in general and precious little about how to help a drug addict. We both knew, of course, that Christ was the answer, but we were only beginning to find out what the questions were. And yet, in spite of knowing as little as I did about the use of street drugs—due to lack of experience and lack of exposure—I felt I knew a lot about the drug addict himself, almost as if this were the one area where I'd had a lot of experience.

And in a way it was. I'd had years and years of experience working with *me.* I'd been dependent on tranquilizers; I'd been a dropout of sorts through my agoraphobia; I'd been inadequate, afraid, and immature; I'd been independent and self-willed. In short, *I'd been helpless.* In those days, if anyone had told me that one day I'd be working among drug addicts, I would have retorted, "If I can just learn to look after myself, I'll be grateful, thank you very much!" But here I was, a few life-changing years later, a whole person and deeply involved with a very special drug addict, with more to follow shortly. This at last was the answer to the prayer I had prayed that painful night so long ago in Geneva. In truth, I had been healed of my helplessness "in such a way" that God was now entrusting me with an opportunity to bring that same healing to others—a healing that could be found only through a life of dependence on God.

But even after experiencing this way of healing for myself, and even after meeting Derek and knowing that he too needed the same sort of healing, I can recall one more occasion when I apologized to God yet again for the fact that I had to depend on Him so much. I had been invited to speak at a meeting near London, which required me to drive in unfamiliar territory during rush-hour traffic. The same old questions plagued me: Will I find my way? Will I get there on time? Will I handle all that traffic? As I entered London, I noticed other drivers whizzing around confidently. I felt I was the only one on the road needing to hope and pray that I'd reach my destination. As usual, because I depended on God, He got me there and home again. Yet I found myself apologizing that I needed to depend on Him so much. Deep inside, it seemed there was still one outpost of independence that saw dependence on God as an unfortunate necessity for a few weak people like me.

No sooner had I voiced my apology than I felt a strong reaction coming from God that I never had felt before, a reaction of righteous indignation. He had had enough of this sorry-to-need-you-so-much mentality, and He wasn't going to tolerate it any longer. Instead, He was going to lay a one-liner on me that would give me a Fatherlike rebuke and a moment of truth all in one: *"You have been* created *for dependence on me,"* He said with absolute authority, *"no apology needed!"*

I knew that if anyone had a right to tell me what I'd been created for, it was my Creator. In spite of all that I had learned so far, I now felt as if I had known nothing until that moment. As the scales fell off my eyes, I understood that this one-liner was not just personal to me, it was universal in application. It was for the strong (so-called) as much as for the weak; it was for men as much as for women.

"That's right!" I said out loud, my mind exploding with enlightenment. "We've been created for dependence— *because* we've been created!"

How had I missed the obvious for so long? *If we had been clever enough to create ourselves,* I sailed on in my thinking, *then naturally we would be clever enough to meet our own needs and solve our own problems. But we have* not *created ourselves*— a ridiculously elementary observation—*we have been created, and by virtue of that creation,* I concluded, *we are at our very best when we depend on Him.*

How fast the mind works when it's been hit with a burst of revelation. My thoughts zoomed back to the Garden of Eden as described in Genesis, and I saw that the "original sin" committed there was none other than independence— woman and then man acting independently of God, bringing about the fall of the human race.

Then I shot forward in my Bible to a verse that I had known by heart for years, Isaiah 53:6. There I saw that independence from God was not only Adam's and Eve's sin, it's been the sin of us all ever since. "We all, like sheep, have gone astray," Isaiah wrote, "each of us has turned to his own [independent] way; and the LORD has laid on him [Jesus] the iniquity of us all" (NIV).

Since it is our iniquity that sent Jesus to the cross, and since the essence of our iniquity is independence from God, then such independence is a most serious matter. And further, since living independently of God is precisely where every human being has gone wrong, then a return to dependence on God, through conversion to Christ, must be its correction. From that day, the day when God opened my mind and elevated God-dependence to its proper place—as part of His original design—I began calling it "the God-dependent life."

But what did all this have to do with Derek and with others like him whom we were meeting on the drug scene? Just this: my understanding now showed me that the answer to their drug-dependence is not independence, though that's what a lot of people assume, and very often drug addicts themselves assume it. No, living independently of God was where they too had gone wrong, just like the rest of the human race. A return to dependence on God would be their correction, their rehabilitation.

Out of that understanding came my own definition of

the drug addict, a broad definition that helped me keep the underlying spiritual problem and the spiritual solution in mind as Bill and I continued in our involvement. (And God was using us both in unique and complementary ways.) Although this definition isn't at all profound, I believe it to be spiritually accurate: A drug addict is someone who, independently of God, seeks to solve his own problems and meet his own needs in his own way.

One thing I appreciate about this simple definition is that it doesn't set the drug addict apart from the rest of the human race, for it is the definition of us all. Any human being who seeks to solve his own problems and meet his own needs in his own way, whether it involves drugs or not, is in fact a *self-dependent* person. He is someone who makes a career out of being self-supported and self-supplied, a career that sooner or later will come into bad times. And kicking that self habit is a lot harder than kicking drugs. Ask any recovered drug addict!

But our God is in the rehabilitation business, of that I became convinced, and His program of inner change (something we all need) is the only one that can deal with self-dependence. It is difficult but possible, I'm sure, for a person to kick the drug habit without Christ—that is, if kicking drugs is all he's got in mind. But it is utterly impossible to kick the self habit without Christ, for self cannot cast out self. Only Christ can do that.

Once more my own life was being reflected back to me through identifying with these youths and through sharing their struggle for wholeness. For the first time ever I recognized myself as a rehabilitated person, restored to wholeness by the greatest Rehabilitator there is and through the greatest means possible—through God-dependence.

So here I was, a rehabilitated person called by God to be an instrument of rehabilitation in the life of another. Never before in my life had I experienced so much agony and so much ecstasy. We loved Derek utterly, and he loved us just as much. But loving him meant that we often suffered pain. This didn't worry me, however, for it was the unconditional love and compassion of Christ within me that made me strong enough to absorb the pain and keep on loving.

And yet, one day I had the scary experience of feeling that I had run out of love. Lately Derek had been letting everyone down. He had let our family down, his own family down, and most of all, he had let himself and God down. He was in London that day with our consent, supposedly on a family visit, but it had turned into a fiasco of rebellion. Finally he called me from London and said a lot of disturbing things. Again, that in itself didn't worry me, for I had experienced this before. What did worry me was my sense of slightly diminished love for him as we talked.

Months earlier, on that train from Reading to Paddington when God opened the windows of heaven over me and poured the compassion of Christ into my heart, I remember feeling that I had enough compassion to last me for the rest of my life. An hour or so later when we met Derek, I felt the compassion of Christ within me move toward him like a well-aimed arrow. Since then, that arrow hadn't shifted in the slightest, not even by a fraction. Not until now, that is.

After laying the phone down, I stood where I was and cried out, "Oh God, is that it? Have I already exhausted your love? If so, I can't go on, Lord. My own love hasn't got what it takes."

In answer, the Holy Spirit immediately brought to mind some very fitting words from James 1:17. I opened my Bible and read them carefully: "Every good and perfect gift is from above, coming down from the Father of the heavenly lights, who does not change like shifting shadows" (NIV).

For a moment I had forgotten that Christ's compassion within me was a gift from above and that there's lots more where that love came from. I also had forgotten that I was only a pipeline not a storage unit. I had forgotten that a pipeline can never run out as long as it remains connected to a supply center. Through Derek's phone call, I had reverted to being a dartboard, and this had wrenched the pipeline away from its source. But the moment I confessed my sin I knew that the pipeline was again open for business. By faith I lifted my life again toward heaven, the one and only place in the universe where there is no shadow of turning nor shortage of love, and I accepted a fresh inflow and outflow of His love and compassion for Derek.

During the next eighteen months our involvement with drug addicts stepped up considerably. On a weekly basis Bill and I would don our jeans and head for London. There we would spend hours, often sitting on dirty floors, talking with the addicted, getting to know them and yes, even respecting them. Drugs could dull and degrade people, but they couldn't erase the traces of God's image in their lives. In all of them we were able to catch at least a glimpse of what they were intended to be, and it was this glimpse that provided a basis for truly respecting them and for calling them back to Christ. A few of them came into a real experience of Christ right there in the filthiest of surroundings. But oh, how hard it was to come back to our sheltered home in Reading and leave them in their hazardous environment. From time to time we would bring someone home with us, and some of our church families kindly helped us in providing homes for them. But these small homes could only accommodate one or two at a time. And anyway, they needed more than loving homes; they needed concentrated and skilled help. In the meantime some of the same young people we had met on the streets of London were dying of drug overdoses.

On one of our visits to London a lovable young man named Danny sought us out and said, "Bill, Joanie, please won't you buy a house in the country so you can help more people like us?" All we could say to Danny was, "We'll seriously consider it." On each subsequent visit he would come looking for us to ask, "Got that house in the country yet?"

One day he sought us out yet again, but this time he wanted us to pray for him. Sitting next to him on a stained and lumpy mattress on the floor, Bill and I had the privilege of leading Danny to the Lord. Then on a later visit he said, "You'd better hurry up and get that house, cuz we're going to die soon." That was the last prodding we had from Danny. Next time we visited London we heard the heartbreaking news that he had died. Because he knew Christ, he now had the joy of life after death, a wonderful eternal reality for him. But he had known nothing of life before death, nothing of the abundant life on earth, which Christ promised and which Danny so craved.

Though Danny had left us, his voice was still speaking, and we were listening. But quite rightly, Bill needed more than Danny's voice to guide him. He wanted to hear from the Lord, not only concerning the idea of a property, but concerning our future ministry. Did the Lord *really* want us in this kind of work, *permanently?* I had already had my word from the Lord shortly before we met Derek. But it was right that Bill should have his own word, and the Lord made sure he got it.

For a number of years Bill had the habit of reading through the book of Proverbs once a month, one chapter each day. On the twenty-fourth day of that particular month, Bill was reading Proverbs 24:11-12:

> Rescue those being led away to death; hold back those staggering toward slaughter. If you say, "But we knew nothing about this," does not he who weighs the heart perceive it ? Does not he who guards your life know it ? Will he not repay each person according to what he has done? (NIV).

Later that day Bill drew me to one side and began to open his heart to me. "Well, this morning I got my word from the Lord," he told me. Opening his well-worn Bible to Proverbs, he showed me those verses. "Funny thing," he went on to say, "I've been reading this chapter once a month for years, but today it really came alive for me.

"You know, Joanie," Bill continued, "there was a time when you and I could have said quite honestly that we knew nothing about this sort of work! But God knows we can't say that any more. And once you know how to do something, I think God holds you responsible to do it and not turn away from it."

One of Bill's many virtues was his carefulness not to jump in too soon. But once he felt it was time to jump, another virtue of his was jumping in with all his might and getting totally immersed. Bill wasted no time doing just that, communicating this new direction to our Operation Concern board members, to our supporters back in the U.S. and to the friends of our work in Europe and England.

By now Derek had moved to a Christian rehabilitation center in another part of England, for he (and we) recognized his need for greater structure and discipline, something we found rather hard to maintain in a cozy family environment. Others who had been living with us also had moved on to other situations, giving us a much-needed lull in our home and family life. In the meantime, there was much to trust God for: large amounts of money and a large property.

The Lord saw fit to show us the right property long before He provided the money, a true test of our faith. Bill had been buying expensive copies of *Country Life Magazine,* always on the lookout for suitable properties. Most of those advertised were too luxurious to consider, and a few were too neglected. Sometimes we drove great distances to view them, but we always came home realizing we were back to square one.

"You know, Bill," I said late one evening at the height of our discouragement, "I think we're trying too hard." He smiled and nodded in agreement. "If God wants us to have a property, and we believe He does, then surely He can make it known to us."

"I think you're right," Bill replied, weary from so much fruitless effort. "Let's leave it with the Lord and see what happens." So we prayed together, rolling the whole matter onto His shoulders, and then rolled into bed with peace in our hearts.

Not too many weeks later Bill came into the living room one afternoon, flopped into his easy chair, and began browsing through our local newspaper. I was in the kitchen peeling potatoes for our evening meal. After a few minutes I saw him get up from his chair and sneak off to his study, carrying his newspaper with him. *Wonder what that guy's up to!* I thought to myself with wifely curiosity.

After a few minutes he waltzed into the kitchen and poked the newspaper under my nose. "See this ad?" he said, directing my attention to a column with print so small you almost needed a magnifying glass to read it. "Yes, and . . . ?" "It's about a property near here, a Victorian manor house on thirty-eight acres of land, and it's just come on the market. I've already called the real estate agent, and we can go see it tomorrow. Oh, by the way," he added with feigned nonchalance, "it's called Yeldall Manor."

"Yeldall Manor?" I echoed with astonishment. "Bill, I've already seen it!"

"I know," he responded with a mischievous grin.

This Berkshire property, located on the edge of Wargrave, was occupied by an American-based Christian community called "The Community of Celebration." I had been taken there one evening by some friends from our church to experience one of their famous praise and celebration meetings. That had been quite a long time ago of course, well before we had met Derek. My abiding memory of the evening was the large oak-paneled room in which our gathering had taken place. At one point, while everyone else was singing praises to God, I found myself looking around the room and cooing inside *This place is beautiful, absolutely beautiful.* I wonder if heaven's angels that evening might have had a hard time keeping God's secret—that one day a few years hence, Yeldall Manor would come into our hands to be used for the Dereks and the Dannys who needed a house in the country, a house of hope and healing.

It was just as well that neither Bill nor I knew what a long haul it would be before we could take possession of this beautiful property and open it as a rehabilitation center— many months of tests and trials of faith, many months of tiring travel and fund-raising, especially for Bill, plus the search for just the right couple to direct the work. At this stage, Bill felt he was not the right person for the job. In any case, he still had more fund-raising to do before he could be free to do anything else.

Finally the day arrived, the day we sometimes thought would never come. In September 1977, Operation Concern officially opened Yeldall Manor as a Christian rehabilitation and training center under the leadership of Cyril and Eunice Evans. This grand opening was marked by a dedication service held in the beautiful oak-paneled room that God had allowed me to glimpse so long before. As a host of friends and community people gathered and rose to their feet to sing, "To God be the glory, great things He hath done," I felt almost faint with wonderment and joy.

Now the real work began! Two years passed, two demanding years for Cyril and Eunice as they pioneered this new work, two years of hard work laying groundwork for the future, two years of sharing the triumph and tragedy of those first ones who came to our house in the country seeking a new life.

And then it seemed time for a change. Cyril and Eunice felt they had completed the task God had called them to do, no doubt the toughest task of all—starting a new work from scratch. By the time they left, however, a solid foundation had been laid for Bill and me to build on, and we were deeply grateful.

And so in November 1979, Bill and I and our two girls, now beautiful young ladies, moved into Yeldall Manor. For the first time since 1964 when our family left Berlin, Bill and I would be working together again, but this time not as Siamese twins. No, this time we would be working *side by side* as two whole people—wonderfully interdependent, yes, but above all, as God-dependent people. And that without apology.

Turning Weakness into Strength

12 How good it was to be a family again. Tina, now twenty-three years old, had been to college, had completed her teacher's training and was back home again. At college she had met Phil, also training to be a teacher, and they were looking forward to their wedding in February. It already had been decided that Bill himself would marry them and that their wedding reception would be held in that historic oak-paneled room at the Manor. Heidi was now a mature seventeen and was still at school. Both our girls shared our deep satisfaction, living and working at Yeldall Manor.

Our apartment was situated at the very top of the house, by far the coziest place to be. The ceilings were low, there were interesting nooks and crannies, and its atmosphere was one of seclusion. These features turned it into a comforting, restorative night-time refuge from the heat of the battle waged two floors below us during the day.

Bill and I particularly cherished our bedroom, a grand looking corner room that cheered us many a morning as the sun sent its first rays through our leaded windows. Each morning Bill would get up first and make mugs of tea for the two of us. Then we would sit in bed together, sipping our tea and feeling like royalty itself.

One morning as we sat there, propped up with pillows and bathed in the morning sun, I remarked to Bill, "You know, the only place nicer than this would have to be Buckingham Palace."

"Buckingham Palace has nothing on Yeldall Manor," Bill said in quick reply, almost as if he had thought it through long ago (and perhaps he had). "The next step up from this would have to be our mansion in heaven!" With that, Bill noticed the time and jumped out of bed with the usual, "Hey, I've got to get moving!"

The work at the Manor had gotten off to a strong start under Cyril and Eunice and those who had worked with them. In those early days we had an average of eight to ten residents, and Yeldall Manor seemed comfortably filled. But since then the work had dwindled to an all-time low. Now we were down to only two residents, and the only staff workers were Bill and me. Money was scarce, discouragement was plentiful, and sometimes we felt as if our work would go under. Not surprisingly, there were a handful of people who thought it *ought* to go under, and they didn't mind saying so. In their thinking, hard times indicated that this work wasn't of God, and therefore we should give it up and let it die. To Bill and me, however, the hard times indicated just the opposite. This was the time to believe God and persevere. And this we sought to do, in complete and utter dependence on Him.

But those hard times were also good times. After a day's work seeking to bring those two residents, "Cowboy" and Andy, one day closer to drug-free wholeness, our family would spend the evening downstairs with them, watching television, laughing and joking with them, playing endless games of table tennis together, and best of all, sitting around a log fire in a cozy alcove, opening our hearts to one another. And how those two residents loved Bill, for he treated them as *men*. Bill never called them "boys" or even "lads." No, whenever he addressed them, it was always, "Ready to go, men?" Or "Okay, men, back to work!" Because of his love and respect for them, they developed utmost love and respect for this big, no-nonsense "dad" of theirs.

Eventually we passed through this lean time, and the work began to build again. But we desperately needed a maintenance man—how well Bill knew it. Bill was many things, but one thing he wasn't was a handyman. As we moved into the winter months, I could tell that Bill was living every day and night in dread of something going wrong in the house—a leaky roof, burst water pipes, electrical faults, oh, a thousand and one things that can go wrong in a rambling place like Yeldall Manor, and no one to deal with them.

Day by day I saw Bill fight off worry through prayer, *urgent prayer* that God would send someone soon to do the job. And it wasn't long until God sent a most surprising answer to Bill's prayer. The man for the job was to be none other than Phil, our future son-in-law! In addition to his training as a teacher, Phil was a "jack of all trades," and a master of them all too. He and Tina felt God was calling them to offer the first year or so of their married life to this work, and they would be moving in right after their February wedding. A few days after this decision had been made, Bill admitted to me that he had gone out into the woods to thank God and to weep with sheer relief. I too felt considerable relief, not only on Bill's behalf, but also for myself, knowing that I would have Tina's assistance in the kitchen and in the running of the house. Even Heidi, though she was still in school, was part of the team. In fact, she got a reputation for her marvelous cakes, which she baked in her spare time to please the entire Yeldall family.

From then on the Lord gave us steady growth in all directions, and no one was going to stop it. Our financial base grew, our number of staff people grew, including office staff, and most important of all our number of residents grew. Even at best, however, the work was costly for everyone involved, but especially for Bill. The pressure of it all was taking everything that he had, and then some, for he not only was responsible for Yeldall Manor, he was responsible for all of Operation Concern.

How grateful I was for the measure of healing that God had accomplished in my life, for at this point Bill needed me to be a God-fearing, God-dependent woman at his side. In those days I could feel him drawing strength and encouragement from me time and again, especially in those early morning hours when we sat drinking tea together in our bedroom. It was during this half hour or so that he would often be feeling despondent over problems and pressures. Then after talking them over and praying with me, he would get his perspective back. By the time he was saying his usual, "Hey, I've got to get moving," he was of good cheer and could be heard whistling in the bathroom as if he hadn't a care in the world. This was the daily renewal that I saw Bill experience day after demanding day.

For me personally, there was nothing I valued more than an opportunity to sit in front of that log fire and chat with whoever came along. With a bit of mending on my lap or perhaps a half-read newspaper, I would be available to listen to incredible life stories being told, hopes and dreams being shared, worries and fears being confessed. And of course, these were opportunities to share and test insights about the God-dependent life.

A young man named John was one of those who liked to slip in by the fire for a talk. On one occasion he stretched out on a sofa next to my chair and stared at the ceiling as he opened up about his problems. "You know, Joanie, I *hate* this dependence problem of mine," he said with emphasis on the word *hate*. "I know I need to become a really independent person, but I can't imagine being dependent on *nothing!*"

"Neither can I," I replied with a smile. "John, has it ever occurred to you that God might have created us to be dependent . . . dependent on something good?"

No, he had never considered that. To him, dependence

was a word with neurotic connotations and it could never mean anything good. Then I reminded him that we are created beings, and because of that there's a natural "dependency tendency" in every one of us that can be satisfied only by dependence on our Creator.

"At first we depend on everything *but* God," I went on, "and sooner or later we find out it doesn't work. So we strive for independence instead, assuming that all dependence is bad. But it's *what* we depend on that makes it either good or bad. I've learned that dependence on God is the one dependence we were made for. When we get that right, we start becoming the people He created us to be."

"Far out!" I heard John murmur. By now he was up on one elbow, his eyes as big as saucers. "I never dreamed it would be okay to be dependent on something. Are you sure about that?"

The best reply I could think of was to tell him my own story about hitting rock bottom, about my battle with agoraphobia, my pill-dependence, and my self-dependence, and about how I was made whole again through God-dependence.

"Wow, Joanie, fancy all that happening to someone like you! I guess you really do understand us guys here at the Manor!"

"But not half as much as Jesus Himself understands, John." By now he was sitting up, and we were relating eyeball to eyeball. I reached for a Bible and opened up to Matthew 11, the last three verses. "Have a look at these verses, John, and tell me if you think Jesus understands. You can read them aloud if you wish. I never tire of hearing them."

I laid my head back and closed my eyes as I listened to him read by the light of the fire those gentle words of Jesus:

Come to me, all you who are weary and burdened, and I will give you rest. Take my yoke upon you and learn from me, for I am gentle and humble in heart, and you will find rest for your souls. For my yoke is easy and my burden is light (NIV).

He looked up from the Bible and said in a soft voice, "Those are beautiful words all right. But I'm not sure I understand them."

"That's exactly how I responded when I read them for the first time. I was a teenager back then and a new Christian. I thought Jesus was speaking mainly to the elderly, to those who were weary from a lifetime of hard work. Then by the time I was in my early thirties and heading for a breakdown, I knew He was talking to all of us, especially to those who are sick and tired of life, no matter what our age is and no matter what our problems are."

"Yeah, that's me all right," John nodded. "I'm really sick and tired." Then he added, "And I'm sick and tired of being sick and tired! Hey, that's rather a good way of putting it, don't you think, Joanie?"

Out of my own experience, I had to agree that it was. "And look," I continued, "Jesus offers us His solution in those three little words, 'Come to me.' But when He says, 'Come to me,' He means for us to come and to *stay* with Him. That's what He's getting at in His next words, 'Take my yoke upon you.' " Then, taking us back to old-fashioned farming techniques, I went on to describe the yoke as a wooden brace that binds two oxen together so that they can plow through the fields together. "The yoke of Christ is similar," I continued, "except it's *Jesus and you* in the yoke, plowing through *life* together, through the easy and the hard of life, through the happy and the sad."

"I'm getting the picture," he replied with a hint of excitement in his voice. Even more moving was the glint of hope in his eyes.

"There's one more encouraging thought in these words, John. Jesus says that when we take His yoke upon ourselves, then we can start *learning from Him.* Just think, it's okay not to know it all! We're allowed to begin again and learn from Jesus how to live life the right way. That's what I had to do, and I know from personal experience that you'll never find a more understanding teacher than Jesus. See, He's telling us that He is 'gentle and humble in heart.' That's because He knows what it's like to be you and me. He lived in skin. He walked this earth. He faced trials and temptations just like you and I have to. And do you know how He coped with it all, John?"

He thought for a long moment and then replied, "I suppose I've always thought that Jesus was able to live as He did because . . . well, simply because He was Jesus . . . God's Son."

"That's true, John. He *was* God's Son. But even as God's Son, He lived His life on earth exactly as you and I are meant to live ours—in dependence on the heavenly Father!"

Now John was looking into the fireplace where the fire had burned down into glowing embers. Did I see tears in his eyes? I wasn't sure. If so, that was between him and God. We sat for a long time, not talking and just letting the truth of God's Word burn into our hearts.

After a while John said good-night and strolled thoughtfully to his room. As I climbed the stairs to our apartment, tired but satisfied, I thought, *"Perhaps I'll soon have the opportunity to tell John about reading, praying, trusting, and obeying."*

And so another day in God's rehabilitation program at Yeldall Manor had come to a close. It had been a good day. Tomorrow might be a tough day, a day full of hassles. But all days, whether good or bad, provided the material God was wanting to get His hands on: *marred clay.* Sometimes that human clay was resistant; sometimes it would grumble, kick, or scream in the Potter's hand. Sometimes that clay would walk down Yeldall's long lane and run back to London or somewhere similar. Just as often it would run back to us. But in the final analysis, it was the marred clay that gave in to the Potter's touch that became whole. And one thing we observed, living in dependence on God had a *normalizing* effect on people's lives. It didn't necessarily make them exceptional, but it did make them *functional,* which is what each person longed to be—functional, like a useful appliance that works exactly as it was designed to work.

On and on the work continued to grow, not so much in breadth now as in depth, which was vital to its future. About this time a new couple joined our staff, Dave and Sue Partington, with their two boys, David and Andrew. Dave, though he had no previous experience working with drug addicts, had a world of experience in management. As the work grew and as the pressure became greater, Bill had been desperately in need of a man with Dave's expertise. It wasn't long until Bill recognized that, sometime in Yeldall's bright future, Dave would be the next director at the Manor. But little did we realize that it would be so soon or why.

It was April 1981. Bill and I had just returned from a trip to Israel in celebration of our twenty-fifth wedding anniversary, and Bill had come back coughing. For a long time now, Bill had had this dry, nagging cough and had been given several courses of antibiotics for it. But no amount of treatment, vitamin C, rest, fresh air, or exercise had made the slightest bit of difference. It was decided that his lungs should be X-rayed. This revealed a slight shadow on his left lung, and so a bronchoscopy was carried out. The results? That unbelievable term—unbelievable when it hits your own family—*cancer.*

The very next day Bill was admitted to St. Thomas Hospital in central London, and several days later they removed the lower lobe of his left lung. Bill came through the operation well, and afterwards, though we hadn't asked for it, he was given a private room that overlooked the Houses of Parliament, Big Ben, and the River Thames. As a lover of political history, Bill was beside himself. Looking out on this postcard scene made him feel as if he somehow had his finger on the pulse of government affairs as he recovered.

The consultant was most positive about the outlook of things. They had caught the malignancy at a very early stage, and later on, when various scans showed no signs of secondaries, Bill was told that he could forget that he had ever had cancer.

In November Bill and I needed to go to the U.S. Not only did Bill have an Operation Concern board meeting, we wanted to visit our parents for the first time since his operation. Since we were in the States anyway, Bill decided to have several more scans done at Mayo Clinic in Minnesota, famous for its cancer research, just to get one last opinion. After the tests, we were relieved to hear that all the results only confirmed the medical opinion in England: Bill could get on with his life and forget all about the big C!

From Mayo, we went on to our Operation Concern board meeting in Chicago, where Bill was able to pass on this good news. Bill looked and felt like a million dollars. And a million dollars wouldn't have made us feel any richer. Then we flew back to England to get into the work again and enjoy a family Christmas. Heidi, in the meantime, had finished school and was now a student at Capernwray Bible School in Lancashire. She too was coming home for Christmas, bringing two friends from Capernwray with her.

It should have been a gloriously happy Christmas for us all, but it wasn't. Within weeks of his clean bill of health at Mayo Clinic, our big daddy was beginning to feel tired, weak, and generally unwell. Even our spur-of-the-moment trip down to warm, sunny Spain did not reverse Bill's downward spiral. When we got back to England ten days later, Bill was worse instead of better.

By now the specialist was getting fed up with Bill's complaints of not feeling well, and he plainly said so. Finally Bill was referred to a Reading psychiatrist, since it was decided that his problems must be psychosomatic. All Bill could say to that was, "I certainly hope and pray they're right." After analyzing Bill for half an hour, the psychiatrist agreed that Bill's problems were indeed psychosomatic. He prescribed sophisticated drugs for Bill's nervous system and instructed him to return in three weeks.

Three weeks later Bill could hardly walk and was in such great pain that I insisted he be seen by someone else, someone other than a psychiatrist. A neurologist in an Oxford hospital was recommended, and the next day I drove Bill over to the Radcliff Infirmary. After only a few minutes of examination, this caring and competent specialist pulled the curtains back and announced, "Well, Mr. Yoder, your problems are not psychological; they're neurological. But I think you may have suspected that already."

"Yes, we certainly did," Bill said, heaving a pained sigh, not knowing whether or not to be relieved. Unfortunately, we had to wait three more agonizing days before a bed was available, but finally Bill was admitted and began to undergo extensive tests. Both of us were determined to find out what was wrong. And we made one thing clear to everyone involved—we wanted the truth.

Finally the day of diagnosis came, and we were asked to come to the consultant's hospital office to talk things over. Bill, dressed handsomely in pajamas and a dressing gown and looking remarkably fit, entered the room first, then I followed. Once inside, I saw the consultant close the door behind me and lock it. That simple turning of the key said it all. I knew what he was going to tell us.

Bill sat in one chair, I in another, and the consultant next to his desk. For one long, deafening moment he sat looking at us with a pained expression in his eyes before he finally found his voice and began speaking.

"Mr. Yoder . . . no words can express how sorry I am to have to tell you this, but the tests have shown that you have cancer—lymphoma. It's terminal, I'm afraid, and there's no treatment available for it—not here in England nor in any other country. We're so very sorry."

"How long have I got?" Bill wanted to know.

By now the consultant was struggling to hold back tears. "It's always hard to say—probably three months to a year."

Bill leaned forward ever so slightly, and with an expression that can only be described as utterly Christlike, said to the consultant, "Sir, my heart goes out to you having to tell us this news." I couldn't believe my ears. My husband had just been given his death sentence, and his first reaction, once he'd gotten the facts, was a feeling of compassion toward the bearer of this news. What a man!

As Bill and the consultant continued to talk over the implications of Bill's critical condition, something was happening to me as I sat there on my chair. From the outside looking in, I appeared concerned but in control. But from the inside looking out, I knew I was starting to fall apart. My joints seemed to turn to jelly, my head was swimming, my stomach and intestines began to feel nauseous and churned up. I felt that at any moment I would fall from my chair in a faint. *I can't be weak now,* came a thought into what seemed like my last moment of consciousness, *Bill* needs *me.*

Still listening to every word being exchanged between the two men, I silently cried out to God from my inner being: *Lord, peace!* Just two words, no more. No sooner had I prayed them than something strange and wonderful began to take place. Something began to rise up in me, slowly but steadily, like mercury in a thermometer. It began in my feet, then crept up my legs and on into my body. By the time it reached the top of my head, I was absolutely all right. I was all right then, and I knew I would be all right from then on—today, tomorrow, and in all the days to come.

Continuing to take in every word being spoken and knowing that I was not drawing attention to myself in any way, I thought inwardly, *I know what's happened to me; I've just tapped into God's grace more deeply than I've ever done before, and that grace is making me sufficient for all that I must face.*

The consultant then picked up his phone and called Mayo Clinic at the hospital's expense, just to get a respected second opinion. He was able to get through to the very person who had examined Bill several months earlier. But sadly, he shared the same grim view, that nothing would be gained by Bill going to Mayo. There was nothing they or anyone could do.

Finally the door to the room was re-opened, and Bill and I walked back to his bed. I pulled the curtains around us, and together we wept without a word in each other's arms. Then, as we dried our tears and tried to regain our composure, Bill said in a flat voice, "Well, what do we do now?" I had nothing to suggest. Then a hint of the old sparkle came back into his voice. "I know. Let's have those two cream cakes that were brought us earlier this afternoon."

So, incongruous as it seemed, I opened the box, and spread out a couple of napkins on the bed and we began to consume those two cakes, licking our fingers and smacking our lips. Halfway through his, Bill commented, "Who but Christians could hear what we've just heard and turn around and enjoy a cream cake?"

Within a few days Bill was transferred to a Reading hospital, and then to another. But neither hospital was equipped to deal satisfactorily with Bill's pain. Then his neurologist called me and said, "Mrs. Yoder, if I were to tell you that there is an available bed at the Sue Ryder Home in Nettlebed, could you get your husband there?" We had heard of this splendid hospice for the terminally ill, and we even had a good Christian friend, Gerri, who did night nursing there. That very day, on March 2, I drove Bill to this stately home. It was a manor house very similar to Yeldall Manor, and so it had the comforting feel of "home" about it. The Sue Ryder Home, widely recommended for its high standard of nursing care, was also known for its expertise in pain control. From his very first day there, we knew that Bill was in the right place.

As each long day came and went, I continued to walk in the good of that all-sufficient grace. By now literally hundreds of Christian brothers and sisters in several countries were holding Bill and our family up in prayer. The elders of our church anointed Bill with oil and prayed over him several times. A well-known healer from the Oxford area made a special trip to the Sue Ryder Home just to pray for Bill's healing. And of course, we as a family, and even Bill himself, were praying for God to heal him.

Each evening I would drive back to Yeldall Manor for a night's sleep, and each morning before driving back to the Sue Ryder Home I would rise quite early to renew myself in the Lord. After making myself a mug of tea, I would sit in a comfortable chair with my Bible on my lap and watch the day dawn across the beautiful Yeldall lawns. This was not the time to get into absorbing Bible study or to make long-winded intercessions. This was a time to say very little and to allow *Him* to speak if He wished, a time to browse through familiar portions of Scripture and simply soak up God's reassurance and comfort.

On one such morning the Lord drew my attention to Hebrews 11, the great "faith" chapter. I began browsing through the stories of some of the Old Testament saints and what they had achieved through faith: some had shut the mouths of lions through faith (I couldn't really identify with that, though I believed it to be true); some quenched the fury of flames through faith (this too went beyond my experience); some escaped the edge of the sword (again something I had never experienced).

But in verse 34 I read of one more powerful effect of faith: ". . . whose weakness was turned to strength" (NIV). Ah, with *that* I could identify! That was *my* achievement through faith *today* in the midst of these dire straits. And in my heart of hearts I knew what enabled me to do it. Gladys Hunt writes in her sensitive book called *Close to Home:*

> I am inclined to believe that special resources are made available to us when we need them, but that our capacity to receive from God and others is determined by the integrity of our relationship to God *beforehand.* A person who has been regularly drinking at the fountain of living water knows where to go when he is parched and dry. Another, used to digging his own well, may struggle to find the path to the Fountain.[1]

A few days earlier I had been on the verge of crumbling in the face of a crisis. But I had known where to go, and I hadn't had to go far. In fact, I hadn't had to go anywhere at all. The Lord and I had been in the yoke together *long before this crisis,* and He was there when I needed Him. All I had to do was stutter my need in His direction, and His strength became mine. Looking back, I've often felt gratitude that He let me taste yet again what I am apart from Christ within me—nothing. That way, anyone hearing this story will never be able to say, "Well, she *would* cope in such a crisis, wouldn't she, since she's such a strong person." No, this story is here to prove just the opposite.

---

[1]*Close to Home* (Grand Rapids, MI: Discovery House, 1990).

Having been reminded of what I was without Christ's life and strength, I was in a position to find out what I could be *with* His life and strength, something I would be proving more and more of in the next few days.

On Thursday morning, March 11, I was driving up the M4 on my way to Heathrow airport to pick up some close American friends who had flown over to visit Bill and me. Suddenly I found myself reaching out to switch on the car radio. *I don't want to listen to loud pop music at a time like this,* I protested. But I disobeyed myself and turned it on anyway. As if on cue, the first sound I heard was a DJ announcing: "Here's 'Annie's Song' by John Denver." Remembering that Bill had chosen this song as an expression of his own love to me and had bought the record for me as a special love-gift, I decided to listen to this one song.

"Come let me love you," the words went, "let me give my life to you. Let me drown in your laughter; let me die in your arms. . . ."

As the words "let me die in your arms" were sung, God gave me the knowledge that Bill was not going to be healed, that he was going to die. At the end of the song I switched off the radio and in the sanctuary of my car traveling at a rate of seventy miles an hour, I prayed a prayer of total relinquishment: "It's all right, Lord. You can have him. He belongs to you. All I ask is, please let him die in my arms."

By now I was staying at the Sue Ryder Home around the clock, sleeping on a couch near Bill during the night. Heidi had come down from Capernwray and also was staying with me at the home. Phil and Tina, having completed their time at the Manor, both had jobs, which meant that they could join us only in the evenings.

On Wednesday, March 17, Heidi and I awoke early and went to Bill's bedside. He was not in a coma, but we had to rouse him in order to get his attention. He wore a black eyepatch over one eye because of his double vision, something he had joked about only days earlier. "All I need now," he had quipped, "is a parrot on one shoulder!" With Heidi at my elbow I leaned close to him and said, "Bill, guess what, today is our twenty-sixth wedding anniversary."

He opened his one eye, and as he focused it on me, it seemed as if warm, liquid love poured out of it. I leaned a bit closer, and he lifted his weakened hands up to my face. With the strength that only love could have given him, he stroked both of my cheeks and said, "I love you, my baby—I love you, my baby." Then he closed his eyes. Those were his last words to me before sinking into the silence of a coma.

That night I went to bed worried that he would die while I was asleep, for I so wanted him to die cradled in my arms. But in the morning Heidi and I were told that Bill had not slipped away in the night, that he was still with us. Since we had had several days of rain and even hail, it was glorious to approach his bed and see the sun streaming across his motionless form. It reminded me of that morning back at the Manor when we sat drinking tea in our sun-bathed bedroom, and Bill had said, "Buckingham Palace has nothing on Yeldall Manor. The next step up from this would have to be our mansion in heaven!"

After fortifying ourselves with a bit of toast and tea, Heidi and I sat down next to Bill. Holding his hand, I studied every familiar line, every precious pore of my beloved's face and listened to his very occasional breathing. I had already decided that when Bill breathed his last, I was going to occupy my thoughts with the fact that his spirit at that moment was flying free of his cancer-ridden body and was soaring up to heaven.

"This is it, Heidi," I said presently, strengthened somehow by the sacredness of the moment. We both stood to our feet, and with Heidi at my side, I gathered Bill's frail, featherlight shoulders into my arms, those shoulders that had borne so much during his forty-eight years, and rested his head on my breast. As that one last, sweet breath passed from his lips, the Holy Spirit gave me the composure to speak over his vacated body the words that I believed with all my heart were being spoken to him that moment at the gate of heaven, "Well done, good and faithful servant, enter into the joy of your Lord."

It was over. Bill was *home* in his mansion in heaven, breathing new celestial air and looking on his beautiful Savior. For a fleeting moment, it seemed as if he had only gone away on another one of his long trips, that after a few weeks of separation he would be back again. *But no,* I thought, yanking myself back to reality and letting my tears flow freely, *Bill won't be passing this way again. I'll be going to him one day instead.*

But until that day, all that I had been taught during our many previous separations would stand me in good stead during this separation. As I now faced the future without Bill, it came to me how thoroughly and how very compassionately God had answered that long-ago heart-question of mine, asked as an anxious young bride: "What if one day I don't have Bill any more?"

God's answer hadn't been the sort that removed all possibility of ever losing Bill, nor had I even expected such a guarantee as that. No, His answer had gone much deeper. Instead of reducing all risks, He had enlarged me and my ability to face them—the only real way of dealing with the many "what ifs" of life. And He had dealt with them "in such a way"—the way of God-dependence—that life no longer had the power to conquer me. Rather, I myself could be a conqueror, *more* than a conqueror . . . *through Him* who loved me.

Epilogue

It would be impossible to end this book without a burst of praise to the great Potter for all His accomplishments in me: for taking up the marred clay of my life and reshaping it so painstakingly, for moving me on from "forced" God-dependence in the beginning to "chosen" God-dependence in the end, for exercising divine restraint and working on my life at a snail's pace. When I add to all this the Potter's willingness to place certain ministries into my fumbling hands even while He was working on my most ragged edges, I am filled with astonishment.

One might ask why God would be "foolish" enough to dare such a risky thing as this. Writer Philip Yancey asks a similar question: "Why does He let us do slowly and blunderingly what He could do in an eyeblink?" In answer to his own question, he then writes: "He holds back for our sake. The motive behind all human history is to develop *us*, not *God*."[1]

This line of reasoning is supported, no doubt, by each one of our lives, mine included. I find it particularly comforting to think that God is not irked by the snail's pace of our progress, but rather *ordains* it for our development's sake, which goes on for a lifetime. Therefore, the end of this book is by no means the end of my story and is certainly not the end of the Potter's efforts in me.

After Bill's promotion to his mansion in heaven, I was left with many decisions to make, both large and small. To start with, of course, even small decisions seemed large— like what to do with Bill's shaving kit, or his clutter on top of the dresser, or his inexpensive but reliable digital watch. I

---

[1]*Disappointment with God* (Grand Rapids, MI: Zondervan, 1988).

remember the day I picked up his watch and stared numbly at those two tiny dots flashing on and off with the precision of a beating heart. Somewhere in the pit of my stomach a hidden-away emotion demanded to know the unknowable: *How is it possible that something as inconsequential as this plastic watch is still going, when something as invaluable as Bill's heart isn't?* That day I was acutely aware of still being on the Potter's wheel.

Then there was the much larger decision concerning my future at Yeldall Manor. Not that I was being asked to leave. On the contrary, the entire Yeldall family—staff and residents alike—wanted me to stay and possibly assumed that I would. But during those early weeks I saw two important reasons for moving out of the Manor and back into the house where Bill, the girls, and I had taken in our first little family of street addicts.

First of all, by leaving the Manor I was freeing myself to get on with the necessary grief-work and adjustments that lay before me, a lengthy process that must not be sidestepped for any reason, not even for the sake of our recovering drug addicts. If I were to stay, I knew I would end up disguising much of my bereavement in protection of these loved ones, for they had enough hurdles of their own to cross without contending with mine.

Secondly, although the Yeldall family wanted me to stay (just as they had longed for Bill to stay), they no longer *needed* either one of us. As Yeldall's pioneer, that's exactly how Bill had planned it—to establish the work and then look for people who could do a better job than we could. Long before his illness, Bill let it be known that he was working toward that day when he could hand the reins over to others so that the two of us might be released to a wider ministry, mainly a traveling ministry of preaching and teaching.

His day of release finally came, of course, though it was painfully different from the day either of us had envisioned. On that day, Bill handed over the reins all right and was duly released to wider service, but not in this world. Instead, through his sad but triumphant death, he was released and raised up to much higher service in God's heavenly realm.

As for me and my future here below, the way forward seemed clear: I was being called, in dependence on God, to follow Bill's vision without him. I was to leave the Manor (though remaining deeply involved) and begin fulfilling the same type of ministry that he and I had hoped to fulfill together.

During the ten years that have followed, this is exactly what the Lord has allowed me to do. In ever widening circles across Great Britain and beyond, He has taken me where I thought I'd never go and has given me a ministry I thought I'd never have—a ministry of carrying the whole gospel to the whole person and discipling men and women in the discovery of the God-dependent life that so revolutionized my own life.

One day not long ago, I strolled over to my bookshelves and pulled out my old, tattered leather Bible, long since replaced by a newer edition, and now held together by a rubber band. I opened it up to that historical first page and began reading my life hymn once more: "Let me burn out for Thee, dear Lord, Burn and wear out for Thee. . . ."

As I read, it came to me forcefully that I was now willing, even longing to let my life burn out for God. With that realization came a strong desire to transcribe the words of that hymn into the front leaf of my current Bible, just as I had done years before in this old one. Sentimental as it sounds, I even wanted it to be in my original handwriting.

No problem! I thought as I carried that brittle, yellow-paged volume over to my desktop photocopier and produced an identical copy of the original words. After trimming away the unwanted edges, I pasted the hymn neatly into the front leaf of my new Bible in exactly the same place it had been in my old.

As I sat down to admire what I had done, I thought back to that rock bottom day so long ago, when I had tried to cut this hymn out of my Bible but had been prevented by the Lord's strong words: "Leave it alone—let me change you instead!" And He had done precisely what He said He would do. *He had changed me.* And here I was years later, still enjoying the results of that change: the wonder of *wholeness.*

For a moment I lingered over the words of the hymn and contemplated their significance. *What does it mean, after all, to burn out for God?* I wondered. *Or what* should *it mean?* I had always believed there was a difference between so-called Christian burn-out and "burning out for God," but I hadn't yet put my finger on it.

In that instant a parable was given to me, a simple parable involving two candles. The first candle was burning at both ends, swiftly and frantically burning itself to death. *That's Christian burn-out,* I thought to myself, knowing that this was hardly what God had in mind for Christians *or* for candles.

The second candle, bearing a tall flame, was on a stand. Two things were happening to this candle as it burned: it was being *used* to send out a warm, steady light, and as it did so, it was being *used up,* slowly but surely.

That's how I want to burn out for God! I thought joyously, more than satisfied with the meaning of the parable. And the meaning seemed clear: according to the parable, "burning out for God" has to do with our earthly lives being *used* and *used up* by God in His service (not used up by sin, Satan, or self, which is what it otherwise would be, for every one of us will be used up by something, good or bad). Then, once used up in a worthwhile way for God, we go on to be *raised up,* like Bill, to higher service above, for it is written in Revelation 22:3, "The throne of God and of the Lamb will be in the city, and his servants will serve him" (NIV).

   With all this understanding in mind I began to reread my life hymn one more time, but this time I made it my "life prayer":

   Let me burn out for Thee, dear Lord,
   Burn and wear out for Thee;
   Don't let me rust or my life be
   A failure, my God, to Thee.
   Use me and all I have, dear Lord,
   And get me so close to Thee,
   That I feel the throb of the great heart of God,
   Until I burn out for Thee.